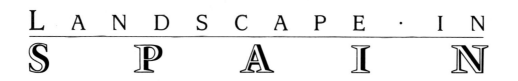

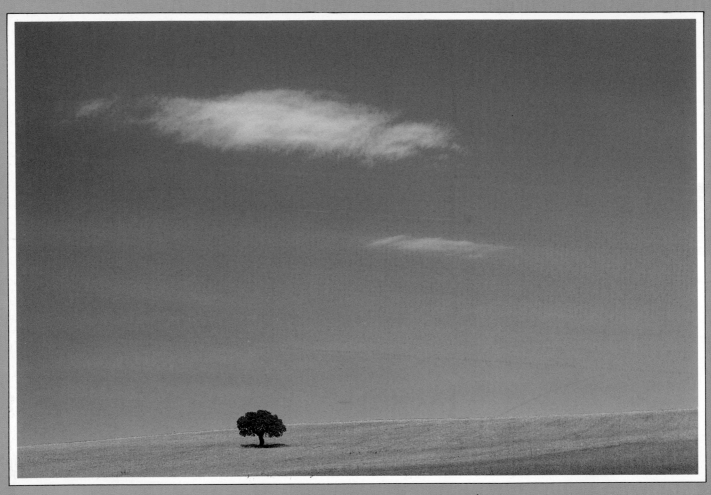

Wheatfields near Alba de Tormes in the province of Ávila

LANDSCAPE · IN
SPAIN

PHOTOGRAPHS BY MICHAEL BUSSELLE · COMMENTARY BY NICHOLAS LUARD

A New York Graphic Society Book
Little, Brown and Company
Boston

Photographs Copyright © 1988 by Michael Busselle
Text Copyright © 1988 by Nicholas Luard

ISBN 0-8212-1706-2
Library of Congress Catalog Card Number: 88-81006

First United States Edition

First published in Great Britain by Pavilion Books Limited

New York Graphic Society books are published by
Little, Brown and Company (Inc.).

PRINTED IN WEST GERMANY

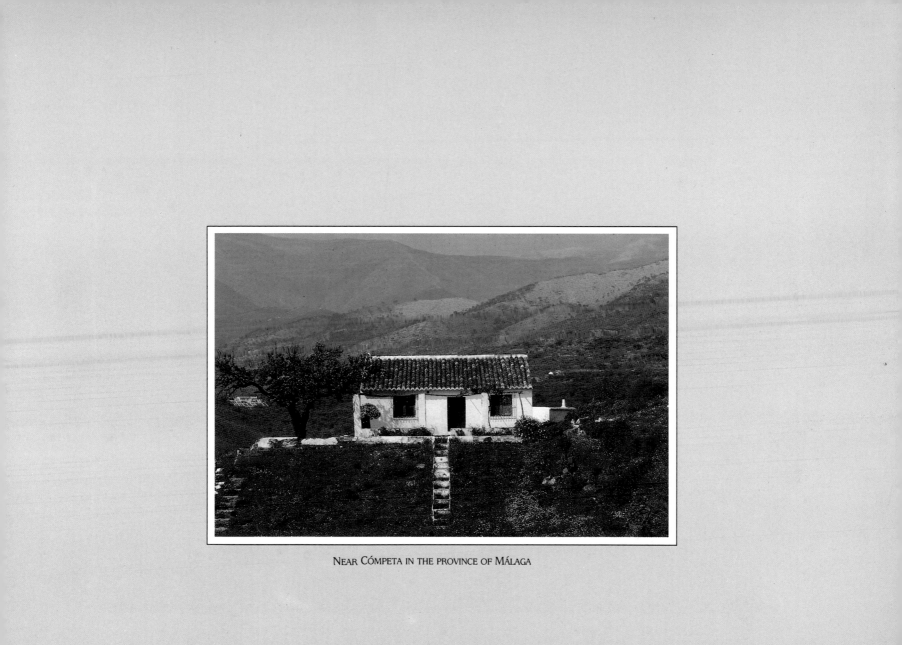

Near Cómpeta in the province of Málaga

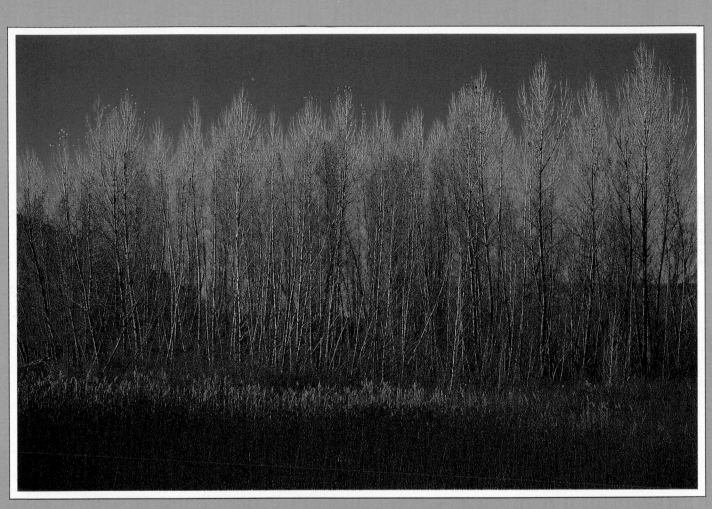

REED BEDS NEAR PRIEGO IN THE PROVINCE OF CUENCA

P R E F A C E

The photographs in this book are the result of about a dozen visits to Spain over a period of three years. I have visited every province and seen the changing seasons and many moods of weather and light. Although I have been a frequent visitor to the country for more than twenty years the detailed exploration of the countryside which this, and another illustrated guide book, *Castles in Spain*, entailed has been a revelation.

It is a land of immense variety. Even within a small area the landscape can change from prairie-like plains to jagged rocky outcrops with small green valleys, secret silvery rivers and wooden glens. Less than an hour's drive, for instance, separates the wheat-covered billiard table of La Mancha from the extraordinary landscape of the Sierra de Alcaraz. Travelling through Spain is an experience which constantly surprises and frequently astounds.

I've gained much more than a fund of travellers' tales and some photographs I'm pleased with however. I've also forged a deeper affection for a country which I had already greatly admired. There are few places to which I've travelled where such large areas of countryside are still untarnished, where rural seclusion is still a natural part of the land.

I have accumulated so many vivid memories that I already have a strong sense of nostalgia. I recall travelling through the Maestrazgo, a remote rocky region in eastern Spain. It was early February and I'd met only a lone shepherd so far that day. The sun was warm and the hillsides were covered in billowing clouds of almond blossom. When I climbed from my car I could hear a suppressed low hum reverberating through the valley. Millions of bees filled the air around me, slanting past at lightning speed. A short while later I sat beside a chill trout stream where dark clear water swirled over smooth boulders. Above a massive wall of rock soared for thousands of feet and I watched a pair of eagles idly resting their great wings on the lilting currents.

There are so many places I want to return to. The majestic Pyrenean valley of Arán which was isolated from the rest of Spain until only a few decades ago. A magical medieval village called Peñalba de Santiago, hidden away at the head of a narrow valley known as the valley of silence. The countryside of the Sierra de Peña de Francía where small stone houses are decorated with wooden balconies from which a blaze of floral colour almost hurts your eyes and cherry orchards shade the surrounding hillsides. I never did see them in blossom. The Sierra de Gredos where springy green turf, tumbling streams and pine forests are guarded by snow-capped peaks.

I long to return to a small valley in Galicia sheltered by the Sierra del

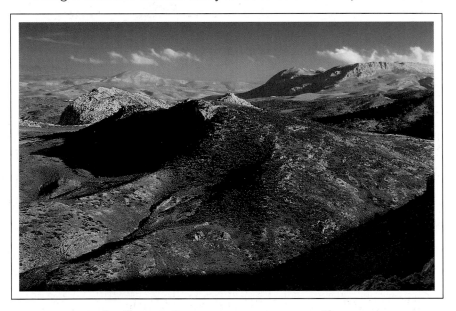

THE SIERRA DE GRAZALEMA IN THE PROVINCE OF CÁDIZ

Suido where paint-box green meadows are dotted with ancient stone *hórreos*. In neighbouring Asturias I recall the small white cottages of Ortiguera clinging defiantly to a wild windswept headland. I remember the canyon of Añisclo near the medieval town of Ainsa. I drove into it late one evening not knowing what I was about to see. The light was not at its best and I left without a photograph but I'll never forget the sense of wonder as the towering cliffs enfolded me.

The impossibly steep meadows lining the valley below the Naranjo de Bulnes in the Picos de Europa is another tantalizing memory, like a half-remembered dream. The journey across the stony track through

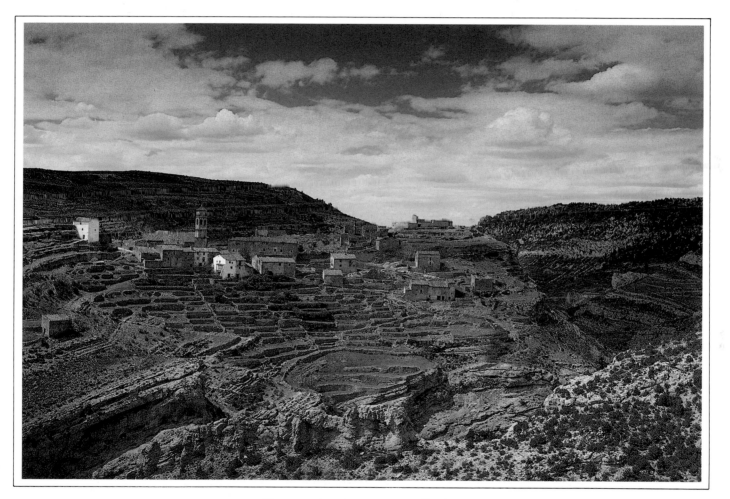

VILLARLUENGO IN THE PROVINCE OF TERUEL

the Sierra de Nevada which leads down into the plunging wooded valleys of the Alpujarras is another memorable experience. An all too fleeting visit to an enchanting village of ragged stone houses called Rupit in Cataluña frequently comes into my mind.

I suppose that working at photography with the inevitable time limits imposed by costs and dealines is actually a blessing in disguise. Like the man who leaves the dinner table before he is fully sated I'm nearly always left wanting more and my appetite for another trip is left keener than ever.

For every photograph I'm pleased with there's a fair few I wish I'd been able to take. Luck plays an unnervingly large role in my working life. I can look at many of my best efforts and realize that had I arrived a few minutes later or sooner I would not have even suspected that I'd missed a great shot. Some are the result of persistence and repeated visits but the ones I'm happiest with are nearly always spontaneous and unexpected.

The photographic process is simultaneously magical and infuriating. Sometimes what should be a great shot simply doesn't quite make it. At other times the foibles of lenses, film and chemistry work like alchemy to give me even more than I'd hoped for. I'm never 100 per cent sure of what I've got.

I have used a 35mm Nikon for all of these photographs. I like the proportions of the 35mm frame best and feel most comfortable using this type of camera. Although I use larger formats in other fields somehow I prefer the photographs I take on 35mm with subjects like landscape and travel. The film I have used throughout is Fuji 50.

I would particularly like to thank Alan Walmsley of Mundi Color for making my travel arrangements and Anne Mapson of Fujimex for keeping me supplied with film.

Michael Busselle

10

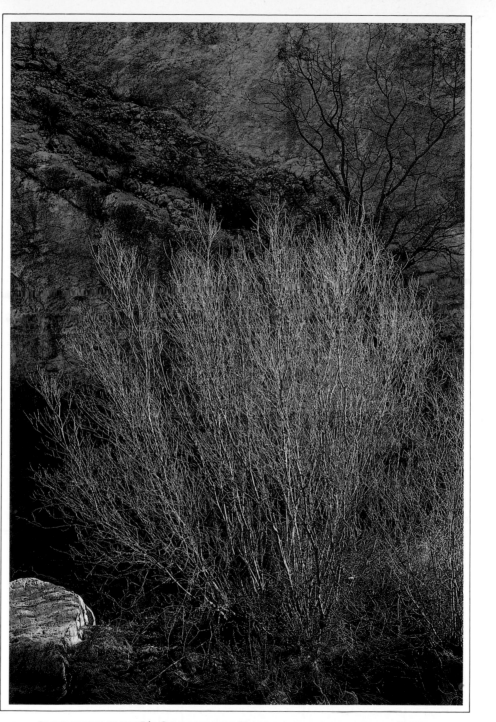

IN THE VALLEY OF THE RÍO GUADALUPE NEAR VILLARLUENGO IN THE PROVINCE OF TERUEL

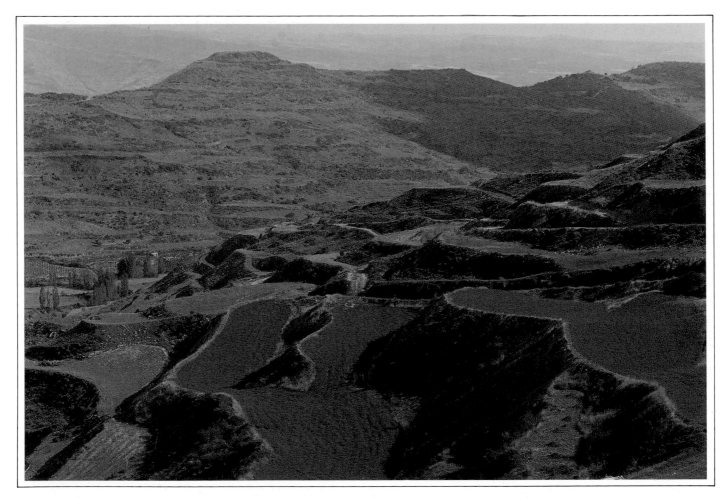

THE VIEW FROM UJUÉ IN THE PROVINCE OF NAVARRA

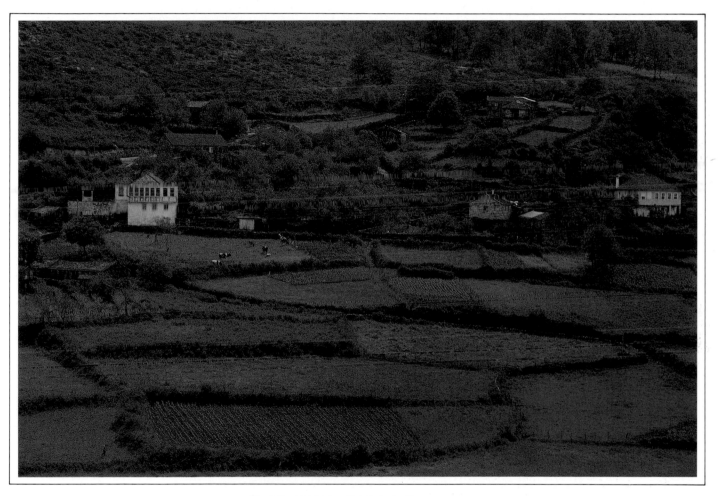

NEAR PINEIRO IN THE PROVINCE OF PONTEVEDRA

13

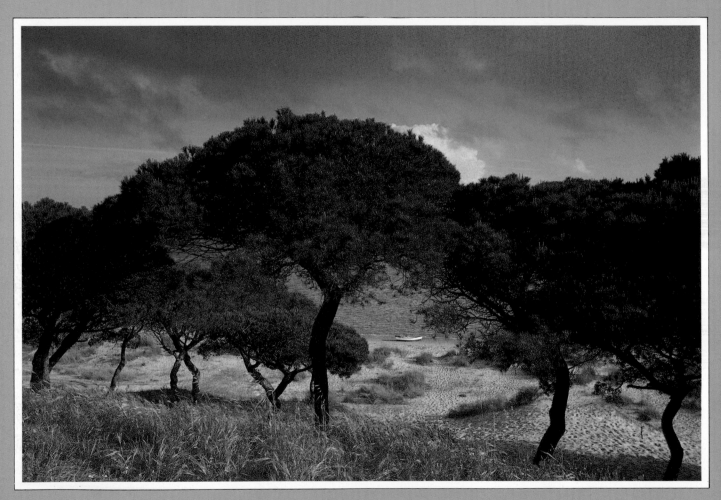

THE BEACH NEAR EL ROMPIDO IN THE PROVINCE OF HUELVA

INTRODUCTION

The house where I lived in Andalucía was set like a great white bird in a glade of a cork forest, at the head of a valley which sloped down to the straits of Gibraltar.

The valley then was a remote and private place. At its foot was a tiny shingled bay guarded by a crumbling Moorish watch-tower. Across the narrow sea-lane of the straits, barely nine miles in width, rose the dusty foothills of north Africa. To the east were the Pillars of Hercules: Jebl Tariq, the sleeping lion of Gibraltar, on the near side, and the matching mountain of Jebl Musa facing it across the water on the African shore. To the west was the little fishing-port of Tarifa. Westwards of Tarifa there was nothing except the grey Atlantic and, somewhere beyond the waves, the Americas.

In winter torrential rain fell on the valley. As the rains dwindled and spring began, a fierce north wind from the sierras behind the house would often blow for days on end. When the wind finally dropped I would set off down through the forest towards the bay. It was no accident the house had been designed as a bird. The straits of Gibraltar are one of the two great migration paths travelled each spring by millions of Africa-wintering birds as they return to nest in Europe – the other crosses the Bosporus at the far end of the Mediterranean.

With the north wind blowing in their faces the birds were kept pent-up on the African coast. As soon as it dropped they erupted in vast aerial caravans to make the sea-crossing. To watch them from the shadow of the tower as they came in head-high in their hundreds of thousands, skimming the shore before beating up over the valley, was for me one of the great rites of the Andalusian spring. It was even more extraordinary to watch the migration from above.

High above the valley and the house was a ridge named the Cabrito, the 'little goat'. From the crescent of tumbling rocks that rimmed the Cabrito I could look down on the vast flocks as they passed, so close I used to gaze from a few feet into the agate-coloured eyes of eagles, hawks, falcons, and the multitudes of swallow-tailed kites. Once I reached out with my hand and brushed the wing of an osprey with my fingers as it swirled by on the thermals rising from below.

The Cabrito ridge was so high that even in summer it was often hidden in cloud. Standing on its ledges, wind-whipped and wind-chilled as glimpses of the valley, the sea, and the African hills appeared and disappeared through the whirling mist, was like balancing on some lofty raptor's eyrie. With the rock falling sheer below it was a dizzying, exhilarating experience – comparable, I thought, to what mountaineers felt on the flanks of the Himalayas or the slopes of the Alps.

The height of the Cabrito ridge is 2,150 feet. It is exactly the average height of all Spain. Wherever the traveller finds himself in that vast country, he is likely – averages being what they are – to be looking out over the Spanish landscape from the same altitude as I did among the migrating eagles on the mist-wreathed rocks above the valley.

Spain, more than anywhere else in Europe, needs a raptor's eye to track and measure and observe. The country is a palace where you are always standing on a balcony among the roofs, a painter from Madrid once remarked to me. He might have added it is a palace with a countless number of halls, chambers, courtyards, and terraces.

When Ferdinand and Isabel finally expelled the Moors from their last stronghold of Granada in 1492 and united the country under a single crown, the formidable royal pair took great care to style themselves not the monarchs of Spain – but of the Spains. Each of the two, of course, was the sovereign of a separate kingdom in their own right, Ferdinand of Aragón and Isabel of Castile. But there were many more kingdoms in Spanish Iberia than Aragón and Castile, and Isabel's shrewd head knew better than to deny the rest of them their dignity and identity in claiming a portmanteau title for the new regime.

The queen was a politician. Acute and successful politicians – and Isabella was extremely acute and very successful – deal in people and realities. To the vast majority of people throughout history the most fundamental reality has always been the landscape that provides them with food, shelter, and a place in which to breed. In acknowledging Spain's different peoples, Isabel was tacitly acknowledging its different landscapes.

Almost five hundred years later, in spite of the convenient single colour cartographers use on their maps, there are still as many different Spains as there were in the days of the Catholic Monarchs. The country remains not so much one nation as a collection of kingdoms loosely

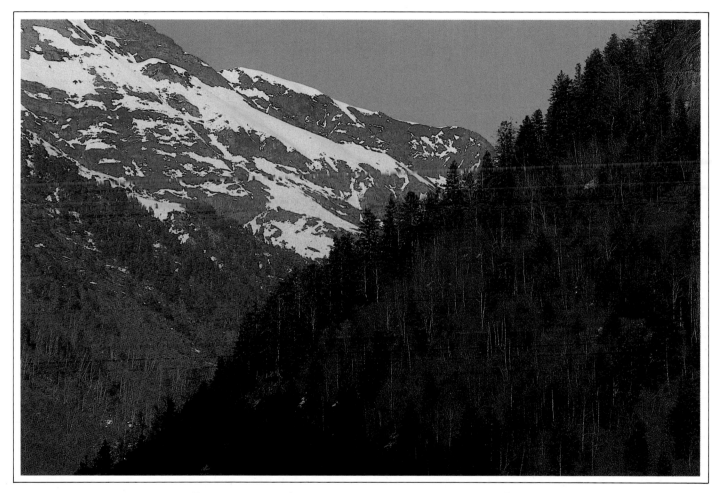

THE VALLEY OF THE RÍO VARRADOS NEAR VIELLA IN THE PROVINCE OF LÉRIDA

joined by a more or less common tongue, Castilian, the language of the 'castles' which evolved behind the line of fortifications raised against the Moors during the long years of the reconquest, and constantly threatening to fly apart – the inherently 'fissiparious' nature of Spain as Franco memorably called it. The separatist movements among the Basque and Catalan peoples are only two of the most strident. Every region of Spain yearns for some form of independence. Within days of Franco's death a great green and white banner was unfurled at the top of Seville's Giralda tower, and the cry of 'Freedom for Andalucía!' rang out over the roofs of the ancient capital – the capital not just of Spain but once of an entire continent, South America, too.

A tapestry of kingdoms in a tapestry of landscapes. Which created which? Did the many obdurate and singular Spanish peoples – Asturians, Andalusians, Basques, Catalans, Galicians – mould the land to their own particular ways? Or did the land, so different region by region that the patchwork of Spain might have been stitched together from different continents, shape them? The effects of the interaction between man and his surroundings are so complex and rooted so deep in the distant past that they are only beginning to be studied. The vast herds of African game, for instance, found by the nineteenth-century explorers did not, ecologists are coming to believe, happen 'naturally'. They were the result of early hunter-gatherer man's discovery of fire, and his use of it two millions years ago to burn the African savannas as an aid to hunting. Firing the grasslands checked the spread of the forests. The animals of the open plains increased at the expense of those of the trees, and swelled to the numbers that astonished travellers like Livingstone and Selous in what was apparently an Eden untouched by man.

Man makes the landscape – but the landscape also makes man. The tension between the two is almost as old as the hills themselves. Nowhere, certainly in Europe, has the print mankind has left on the face of the land been quite as robust or varied as in Spain. All of human history reduces in the end to the history of food. Without it there is neither sex nor art, politics nor warfare, civilization nor barbarism, past nor future. The kingdoms of the Spains are nothing more – and nothing less – than a coming to terms in different ways with man's need to fashion granaries, gardens, and larders out of his home earth. Because the landscape was there first, the landscape had the first word.

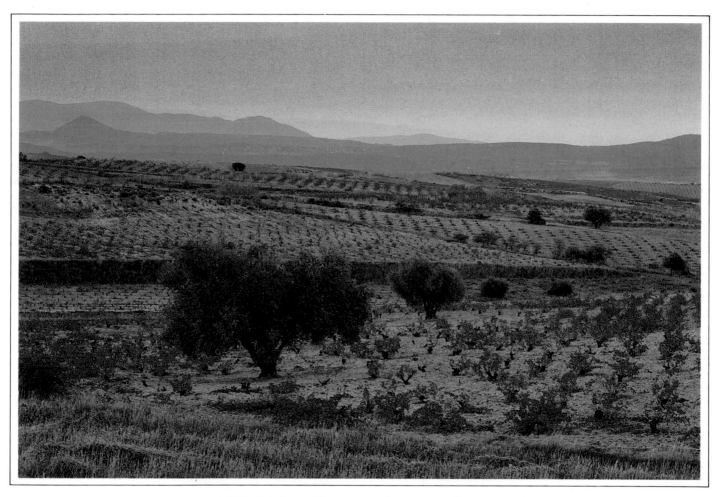

THE VINEYARDS OF MENTRIDA IN THE PROVINCE OF TOLEDO

19

'Europe ends at the Pyrenees' was another of the little general's favourite maxims. On one level Franco was speaking with the politician's voice of his long-ago predecessor as ruler, Isabel. The turbulent Spains, he believed, were not suited to the democratic systems of the nations to the north. On a deeper level he was referring to something in the Spanish spirit alien to the rest of Europe, a daemon engendered in the land. The immense palace he seized at gun-point was not only built on mountains. Its uniqueness, its sense of apartness, its isolation from the rest of Europe, was nurtured over long centuries behind the towering barrier of its most intimidating mountains – the ramparts of the Pyrenees.

For the modern visitor, who can land from the skies at any one of a dozen major airports scattered across Spain, it is difficult to grasp quite how daunting the Pyrenees were – and still are – to those who had to travel them by foot. In winter they are still impassable in many places for months on end. Even in summer in the age of the motor car, as anyone who has slowly wound their way up the pass of Roncesvalles knows, they remain a challenge – and experience to be greeted, as the road eventually crests the peaks, with relief and a sense of achievement. For thousands of years they walled out the known expanding world; even Spain's brief period as a European colonial power failed to breach the physical and psychological remoteness of the countries to the north. When a Spaniard lifted his head from the palace grounds and looked afield, he turned in the opposite direction. He gazed away from Europe towards the south.

He still does. From Spain the natural perspective has always been different. The European looks west to north America, or east to the brooding presence of the Slavs on his borders. Not the Spaniard. The lie of the land directs his eyes towards Africa. From out of Africa, from across the channel that lay below my house in the valley, have come most of Spain's nightmares and many of its treasures. And if his eyes do swing westwards, the limits of his gaze stop short of the United States. They encompass only his lost empire, the mountains and jungles of Latin America from where, fleetingly, even more dazzling riches than the Moors bequeathed were to be had as plunder.

Mountains frame and define the Spanish as no other European race. Only little Switzerland has more of them and Switzerland's circumstances are different: bordered on every side by other nations, Switzer-

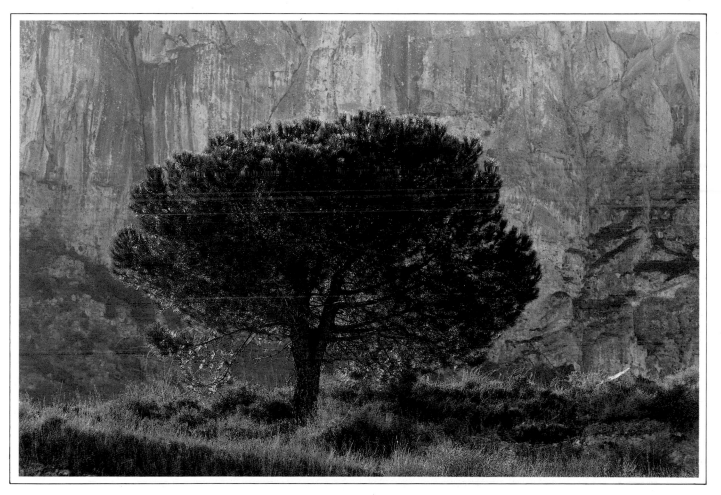

NEAR CASTELLOTE IN THE PROVINCE OF TERUEL

21

land has always kept windows open to the rest of the world. What the two countries have in common, and it is no coincidence they do, is that both of them have always produced Europe's finest soldiers and mercenaries. Mountain gardens and granaries are notoriously difficult to hew out from the rock. No wonder that their guardians, like the Gurkhas, make such fearsome warriors – or that Spain gave the word 'guerrilla' to the international vocabulary. To the Spanish the Pyrenees have been both prison bars and a mighty portcullis which has kept the undesired world beyond the walls. But the Pyrenees are only one of the mountain chains which dominate Spanish existence.

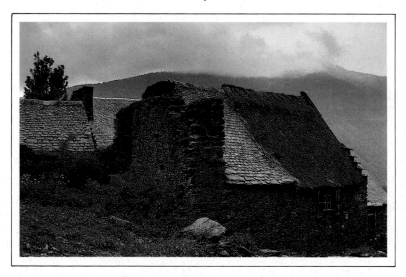

BAUSEN IN THE PROVINCE OF LÉRIDA

At the heart of the country is the Meseta, the vast central plateau which in its turn is barricaded with upland ranges – the ring of the Cantabrian and Iberian Cordilleras running from west to east, and the Sierra Morena, the cloudy oaken and chestnut-brown mountains, to the south. The mountains do not even end there. Further south still are the Sierra Nevada, the hills of the snows, crowned at 11,211 feet by the country's highest peak, Mulhacén. Wherever one goes in Spain, along whatever high gallery of the palace one wanders, the presence of land higher still is always close.

If the landscape makes the man, and the higher the landscape the harder the man, then mountains also impose their own discipline not

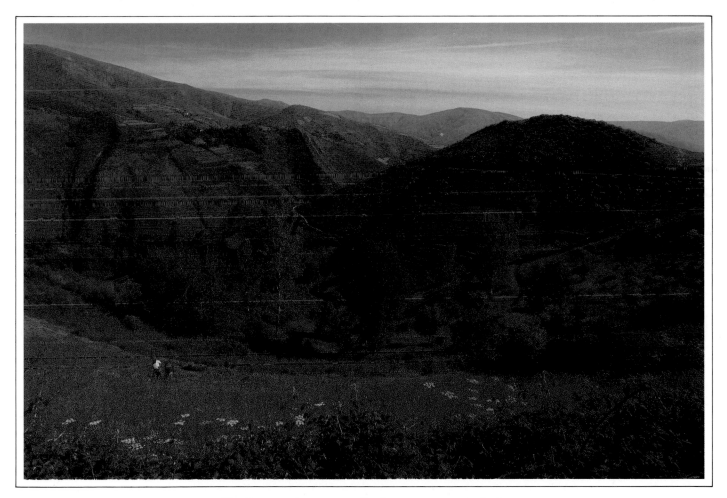

THE SIERRA DE ANCARES NEAR DONÍS IN THE PROVINCE OF LEÓN

just on the individual but on the group. Huge areas of upland Spain are uninhabitable from lack of water, or because they lack soil good enough to support crops or herds. Where a living can be wrought from the hills, it is often only in scattered pockets of land. Until recently communications in the remoter regions were virtually non-existent. Each village was almost a nation, a world, of its own. Even today two little white-walled settlements in the sierras, facing each other across a valley, will use quite different words for a whole range of everyday objects and activities. Ferdinand and Isabel might with equal correctness have called themselves the Monarchs of the Pueblos, for all that the thousands of Spanish villages have in common.

The hermetic life of the isolated little pueblos has traditionally bred pride, passion, stubbornness, and ferocity – the archetypal traits of the Spanish character that such different observers as Richard Ford and Federigo García Lorca recorded. The picture has a fair measure of truth. But its source is not in the genes, it is not something uniquely and quintessentially 'Spanish' as writers going back far beyond Ford or Lorca maintained, and many Spaniards, seduced by the romantic qualities of the image, believe. It comes instead from the impress of the brutal and unforgiving land. Wherever people band together in remote and hostile uplands they tend to develop the same traits. The Pathans of the Kyber Pass, a world apart in race, culture and geography, have similar values and characteristics.

The hills dictated where the early Iberian felled the trees and put his hoe to the soil. From that moment on the Iberian – Andaluz, Catalán, or Galician – took over and tried to put his own signature on the ground. The peoples of the Spains have much in common with the highland Scot, but unlike the Scot the Spaniard is instinctively a social and urban creature. To the highlander his house, whether a croft or a castle, is merely a temporary shelter. His real home and living-space is the 'hill', the heathered moors, the peaty burns and rivers, the barren high tops. The Spaniard is the opposite. His hearth and home, the centre of his being, is beneath *his* roof in the tightly-packed cluster of buildings of *his* pueblo. The land beyond is simply the raw material of agriculture or herding – and the further it stretches from the pueblo, the less attractive it becomes. (The word pueblo has several meanings – it can be used for any human grouping from the tiniest hamlet to a city to an entire nation – but it always implies a sense of community, of shared identity.)

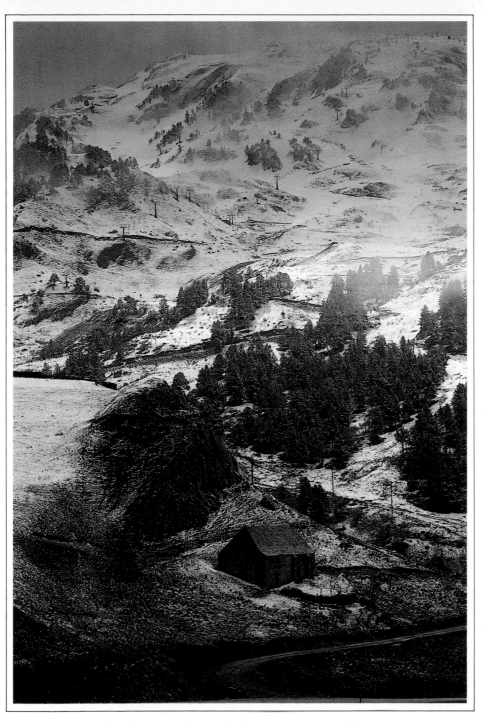

THE VALLE DE ARÁN NEAR ARTIÉS IN THE PROVINCE OF LÉRIDA

One result of the Spaniard's obsession with the pueblo is that he will always work the land as close to the village as possible. Very often there is no choice. The original settlement will have been made because only the surrounding earth, and no other land close by, could be tilled. But where he can choose between laboriously building terraces on an almost vertical hill just above the pueblo, or cultivating flat, and perhaps richer, land only a short distance away, the Spaniard will always opt for the former. No extra yield or easier labour can compensate for the immediate and comforting presence of the village.

A palace guarded by mountains, built on mountains, and thronged by mountains, with its multitudes of little isolated granaries, gardens, and larders – the white-walled pueblos made by the hard men of the many Spains – scattered among the clefts and ravines like drifts of fresh-fallen snow. That in many ways is upland Spain. The seemingly immemorial whiteness of the villages is in fact less than a hundred years old. The virtues of lime-washing, which produces the glowing matt-white skin on walls, lintels, and door-steps, had long been recognized in the south, but it was only in the nineteenth century that a government decree made its use obligatory all over the country on grounds of health. In some places like the Alpujarras mountains, the law remains ignored and the grey stone pueblos blend into the hillside as they have always done. The uplands, the hills and mountains and the plateaux that link them, dominate the land. Yet as well as its parapets and balconies, the palace is festooned with gardens, fountains, and courtyards on its lower floors too.

Much of Spain is arid. The climate of the great raised table of the Meseta is described by its inhabitants, the Castilians, as 'Nine months of winter and three months of hell'. The Meseta is cut off from the effects of the seas on either side by the barriers of its surrounding sierras. But in all the temperate zones of the world, wherever there are mountains and the sea clouds can reach them, it follows as the night follows the day that there will be rain. Spain being Spain, in those parts of the landscape where the rain falls, it cascades down in vertical black cataracts and torrents that make the rainfall of the traditionally damp countries of northern Europe appear like passing showers. Even in the far south of Andalucía the winter deluges can be so dark and heavy that candles are still sometimes burned at midday in every house in the valley: without their light it is impossible to see across a room. Pouring

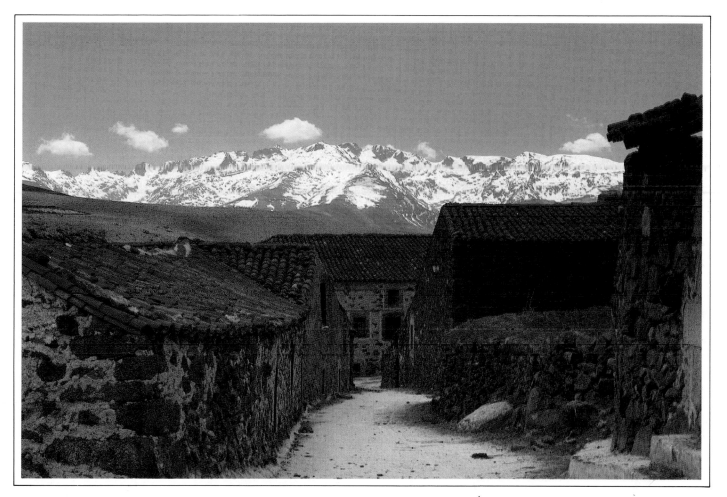

Las Herguijuela near Piedrahita in the province of Ávila

Near Candeleda in the province of Ávila

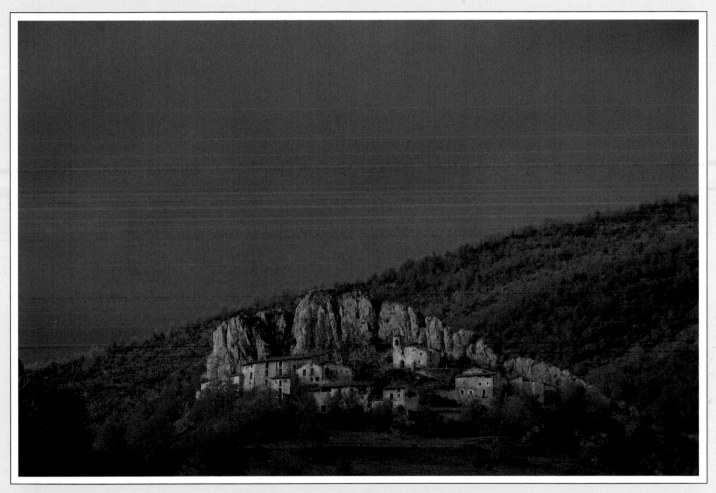

Near Pont de Suert in the province of Lérida

off the hillsides, the country's streams twine together and sweep their way back to the sea down a thousand water-courses. Among them are Spain's five great rivers. Only one, the Ebro, drains east into the Mediterranean. The other four flow westwards towards the Atlantic.

The mightiest of the four and the one which has had the strongest effect on Spain's history, is the Guadalquivir. Rising high in the Sierra de Cazorla, the Guadalquivir flows down to its mouth in the Atlantic among the Marismas – the great wild marshes of its delta to the south of Seville. Columbus set sail from the Guadalquivir. Throughout the sixteenth century its lower reaches were travelled by the galleons carrying back the seemingly inexhaustible metallic river of gold from the New World, making Seville for a while the richest city on earth. For centuries before that, and for long afterwards, the harvests from the fertile inland plain of the Guadalquivir's huge valley were the largest gathered from all the prairies which stocked Spain's winter barns.

Not far to the south of where the Guadalquivir rises lies Granada. Watered in part by streams from the same mountains that feed the Guadalquivir, the plain that surrounds Granada, the *vega*, is all of the great river's wealth in microcosm – and richer still. The *vega's* earth is so fertile, its rains so regular, its sun so clear and warm, that the plain can produce three crops each year. The mountain Arabs from the bleak and bone-dry foothills of the African Atlas were seduced into invading Andalucía by tales of the land's constantly-running water. When they reached Granada and discovered the *vega*, they found the tales were true. They pronounced the city and its plain the ante-chamber of paradise, and settled down to colonize it for eternity. The Moors' Spanish adventure cost many a caliph's ransom, but they had a good run for their money. Their eternity lasted almost eight hundred years. In the end they reckoned without the hard men from the north and the two ambitious monarchs who broke down the gates of the Arab citadel at the head of their castle-language speaking troops.

If the bleak plains of La Mancha represent the Spains at their harshest and most inhospitable, and the Guadalquivir valley or Granada's *vega* represent them at their most fruitful and benign, the climates and landscapes remain essentially their own. The scouring winds and bone-chilling frosts of the plateau, the red soil of the *vega* – so fecund that seeds germinate within hours of being pressed into the warm moist earth – were there before man came. Their landscapes largely formed

30

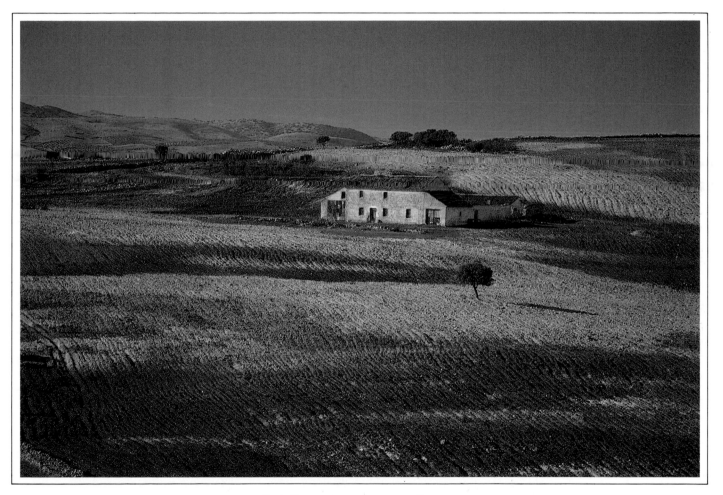

31

NEAR GUADIX IN THE PROVINCE OF GRANADA

the people who settled them. What of the tug from the other end of the rope – the tug of man on Spain's land?

Madrid lies at Spain's centre. Decreed the country's capital by Philip II as recently – in terms of the country's history – as the sixteenth century, no seat of government could have been placed more exactly in the middle of the nation its monarch ruled. Like many rulers Philip II decided to give the capital and his regime an emblem, a banner so identifiable that all who saw it would know instantly what place – and what power – it represented. The most easily recognizable symbols of

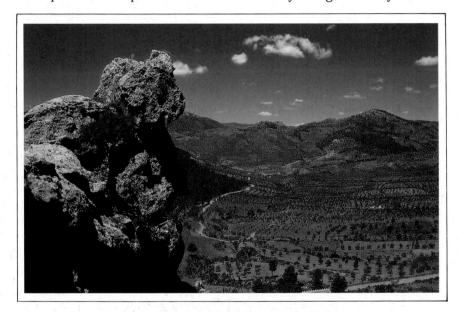

NEAR BOGARRA IN THE PROVINCE OF ALBACETE

any place are the most typical and familiar. For Madrid Philip chose a bear in a forest thicket, the forest's trees being *madroños*, the wild strawberry tree which flowers one year and fruits the next. No one who saw Madrid's banner and knew the area could fail to associate it with the capital.

There are still a few bears in isolated parts of the Spanish mountains, and in its fruiting years the Andalucían gypsies still sell the scarlet *madroño* berry, wrapped in cones of sugar paper, as a treat at the autumn *ferias*. But for hundreds of square miles round Madrid both the bear and the *madroño* have disappeared. Just as in the Scottish

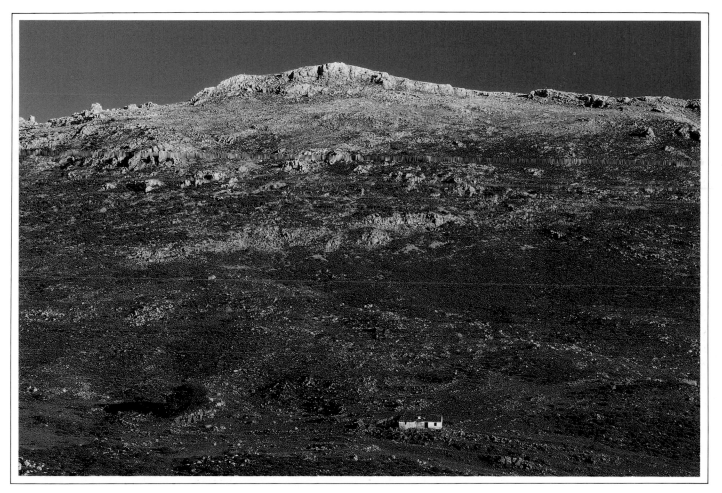

33

Near Ronda in the province of Málaga

highlands, where only a few hundred years ago the now heather-clad hills were covered with the Caledonian forest, the land has been stripped bare. The phenomenon of the vanishing forest is not merely a European tragedy. It has become a world-wide one. Very occasionally, given changed circumstances, luck, and time, the trees will eventually grow back. Much more often the destruction is irreversible.

In Scotland the red deer, the rabbit, and the flocks of highland sheep, are now so widespread that however many tree seeds germinate, the forest cannot regenerate itself – the seedlings are eaten long before they have a chance of maturing. In Spain the outcome is the same, although the causes are different. The forest canopy which bound together the bears and the strawberry trees also held the soil in place. When the trees were chopped down the soil was simply blown away by the bitter Meseta winds, or washed away under the assault of the winter rains. The pictures in Madrid's Prado museum show some of the richest and most sensuous natural European landscapes ever painted. They hang within an hour's stroll of a man-made desert.

Today it is fashionable to call forest-felling – or, often equally as ruinous, the planting of alien trees on battery-farming principles in wholly inappropriate landscapes – improved or more efficient use of the land. Almost every word in the justification turns the normal meaning of language on its head. There is no improvement, only accelerating deterioration. No efficiency, only waste. There is not even use, only destruction. But periodically throughout history areas of land colonized by man have been stripped of their natural mantle of vegetation and put to a different purpose, without necessarily eroding the soil or reducing the countryside to a dust-bowl. Round the Mediterranean it has happened in the case of the olive and the vine, although they have all too often been accompanied by the appearance of that fearsome engine of plant destruction, the goat.

The olive arrived in Spain with the Romans. For several hundred years most of Spain was part of the Roman empire; the emperors Trajan and Hadrian were both Spanish – or more accurately Andalusian-born. Like so much else the olive flourished in the Iberian soil as nowhere else. Although Tuscany, Provence, Greece, and a dozen other regions of the Mediterranean claim to produce Europe's finest olive oil, when it comes to the fruit itself the palm has always been awarded to the olives of the silver-green trees which throng the plains and hill-flanks of so

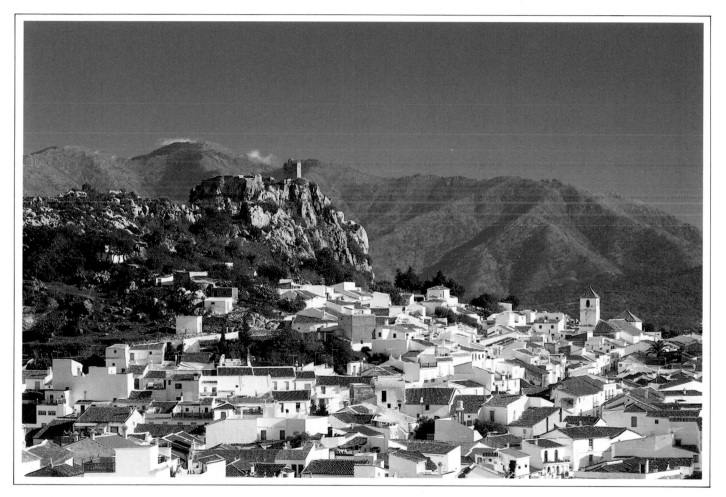

GAUCÍN IN THE PROVINCE OF MÁLAGA

much of the Iberian peninsula. With the Romans, too, came the vine. Spanish red and white wines have seldom won the acclaim that at their best they deserve, although the deep oaky reds of Rioja are finally being recognized for what they are – the cleanest, sturdiest table wines with the longest pedigree, apart from those of Greece, in the western world. The golden wines from the chalky soils round Jerez, 'sherry' in the anglicized corruption of its name, have had no such problem; they have always been known to be peerless.

Wheat reached Spain long before the Romans, probably with the first waves of migrants who brought with them the seed-stock their ancestors had raised in the Jordan valley. Once again the Romans realized that like the olive and the vine, some strange alchemy in the Spanish soil made the wheat grown there different from any other in the empire. From Hadrian's wall to Rome itself, Spanish bread was known as the best in the world. Below the white bird of my house in the valley was a small peasant bakery with a primitive wood-fired brick oven. Out of it came loaves unlike any I have ever tasted. In the hand they felt as heavy as oak. Floury and hard-crusted, a rare blend of flint-grey and beechmast-brown in colour with a dense pale creamy crumb, they kept without mildewing not just for days but for weeks – and always without losing their flavour. They were loaves which could be carried by the cork-stripping gangs on long expeditions into the wilds of the sierras. A month out of the oven they would be as good as when the sparks from the fire were still sizzling on their rounded flanks. A centurion, who had been posted to the Baetic province and then transferred to a garrison in the far north of the empire, wrote home wistfully that what he missed most, apart from the eternal city, were the loaves of Andalucía. In two thousand years nothing has changed.

The olive, the vine, the seed of Jordan valley's durum wheat – they have all changed the face of Spain's landscape almost as much as the felling of the forests. Like the red deer and the rabbit in the Scottish highlands the goat, an even more athletic and versatile feeder, ruthlessly perpetuates the consequences of the changes in the land's use. Where the goat climbs, not only will nothing grow back, even the scraps of the original vegetation that remain after the land's clearance are in peril. Spain bears the goat's scars, but it can live with them as it lives with other newcomers. Something like one-sixth of the country now produces maize. Maize arrived from the New World like the potato less

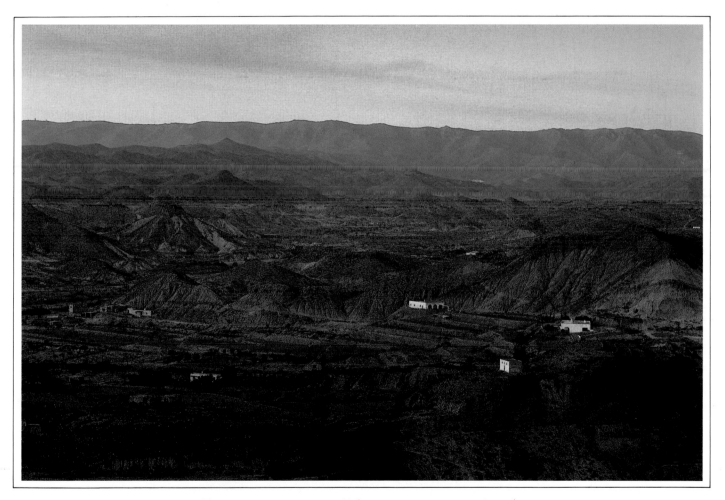

THE VIEW FROM THE CASTLE OF TABERNAS IN THE PROVINCE OF ALMERÍA

than five centuries ago with the returning *conquistadores*. Even in human chronology five hundred years only span twenty generations: in the lifetime of a landscape they are barely an eye's blink. Yet within that time an area larger than England has been handed over to the cultivation of an alien corn.

The almond orchards, whose white blossom mists the Mediterranean coast in spring from Seville to the French border, came with the Moors. The Arabs were famous for their sweet tooth all over the early medieval world. In Spain the trees live on in their thousands and the Moors' delight in sweetmeats survives in *turron*, an almond nougat eaten everywhere as a celebration of the twelve days of Christmas. On the irrigated plains of Valencia the rice yield – rice is yet another foreigner – is the highest per acre anywhere that the crop is cultivated, far higher than in the paddies of Asia. Not all the man-made changes have come in the form of new plants or animals. Some have been subtler, less obvious in their effects and more apparently 'natural'.

One of the earliest and most basic rights of the herding peoples of the Spains was to move their animals without let or hindrance between summer and winter pastures, the ancient practice of transhumance. As a flock or herd can only move at the speed of its slowest member, transhumance is a lengthy business. On the journey the animals have to eat. The *caminos reales,* the 'royal roads' as the old rights of way are known, had to be broad enough to provide grazing for the animals which travelled them. Grass will not grow in the shade of trees. So great swathes were cut through the forests and protected on their routes across the plains and hills to allow pasturage to develop. The open sunlit *caminos* were invaded not just by grasses, but by a whole host of flowering plants from orchids to wild narcissus to rare anenomes. They include several species which, having been killed off by pesticides and modern agriculture methods elsewhere, now only survive along the network of transhumance tracks. The wildflowers of the Spanish spring are one of the countryside's shining glories. But the huge drifts of rippling colour the traveller now sees may well owe little to the ancient landscape, and much to the obdurate Spanish herdsman, the long-ago guerrilla of one of the many kingdoms, who demanded free passage for his animals – regardless of any territorial privileges claimed by king or nobleman.

Burning is another human activity which affects the face of the

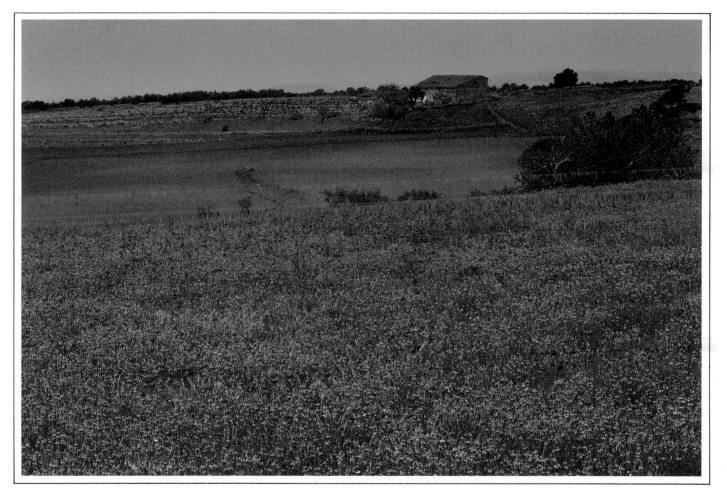

NEAR PUERTOMINGALVO IN THE PROVINCE OF TERUEL

land. Like the African hunter-gatherers, the early Spanish discovered that if they set fire to the layer of last season's dead vegetable matter, a mat that kept the sun from the soil, the earth beneath would be stimulated into sending up new growth. As an aid to forcing crops and pasture it has been used for as long as the Iberians have worked the Spanish landscape. Although less common today than it was, many rural Spaniards, including notably Spain's gypsies, still burn the land to bring on wild crops like asparagus and mushrooms – which can either be eaten or sold for cash in the country's markets. Wherever the columns of smoke rise above the *mattoral*, as they do day after day for months, the countryside is being altered. The seedling trees are being scorched, the dense scrub is little by little being pushed back, holes are being ripped in the vegetation mantle. Grasses and wildflowers will invade the cleared spaces that grow larger year by year with fresh fires. With them will come tiers of insects, birds, and animals – all feeding off or co-operating with each other. The final result will still be an acre, a half-acre, of Spain, but it will be a different acre or half-acre from the one that stood there before. The landscape will have changed, and the instrument of change will have been man.

Landscape makes the man – man makes the landscape. Caught up inevitably in the relationship between the two are the animals and birds of the wild who were there long before the abrasive flux began. One day soon after I began to build my house in the valley, I was walking through the forest when I saw a strongly-built animal the size of a small fox trotting towards me along the winding goat-path. It came up, sniffed fearlessly at my boots, and moved on about its own business. The animal was a mongoose. Mongooses are usually associated with Africa or India, and I have even known naturalists surprised to learn they can be found in Spain. There is only one European population of the courageous and immensely powerful little animal, and it lives in Andalucía. Over the years I came to know the mongooses of the valley well. When I first came there they were common. So were foxes, badgers, genets – slender black and white striped wild cats – and in the stream of the Guadálmez that ran down to the straits, terrapins which used to sun themselves like drowsy bees on the rocks that rose from the pools. By the time I left fifteen years later in 1980 they were all in retreat. The water pumped from the Guadálmez had reduced the river to a trickle, the spiney maquis was being cleared for development, the old

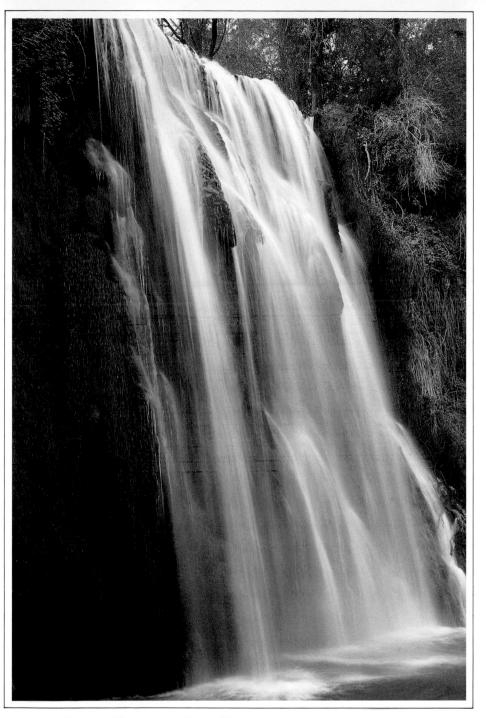

NEAR THE MONASTERY OF PIEDRA, NUEVELOS, IN THE PROVINCE OF ZARAGOZA

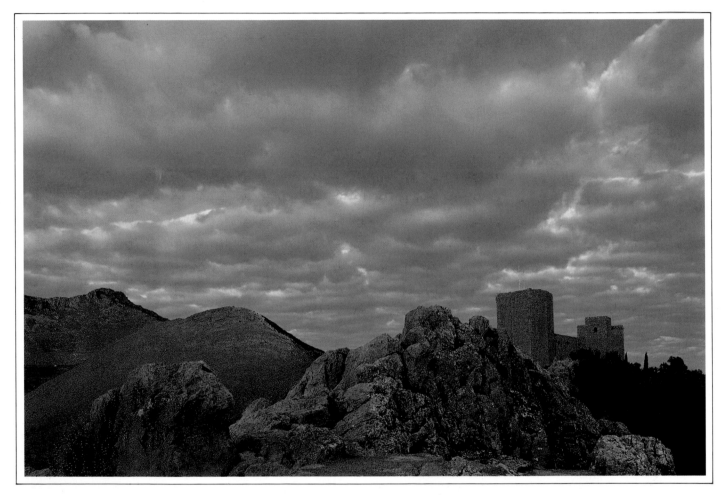

The castle of Santa Catalina, Jaén

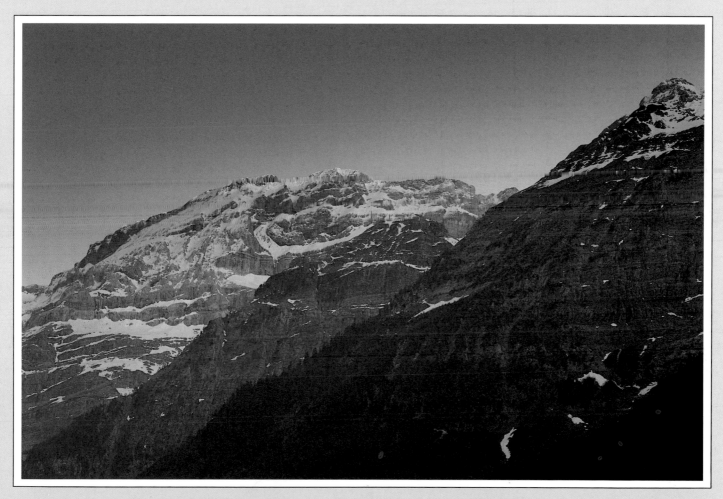

MONTE PERDIDO SEEN FROM THE VALLE DE PINETA IN THE PROVINCE OF HUESCA

and intricate wilderness living-space, thick with the scents of resin and pollen, was being destroyed.

Most of Spain's wolves have been a casualty of the same process. Writing of his life in the 1920s in the village of Yegén in the Alpujarras mountains near Granada, Gerald Brenan tells how in winter it was common for a caged wolf, trapped somewhere on the hill-flanks above, to be brought down into the village square and displayed to the inhabitants. Now wolves are only a vague and uncertain memory among the very old of the Alpujarras. Bears have gone the same way as

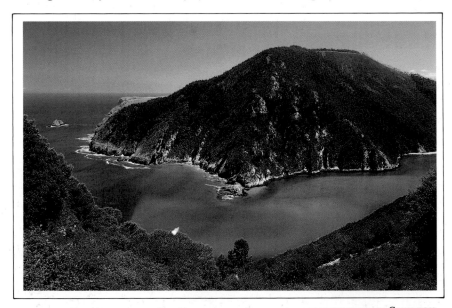

THE RÍA DE TINA MENOR NEAR SAN VICENTE DE LA BARQUERA IN THE PROVINCE OF CANTABRIA

has the wonderful Spanish lynx, the elegant tawny-skinned predator of the hills and plains. The Spanish Imperial eagle – as majestic as its name – has been reduced to a few pairs. Vultures, the great cleansing machines of the sierras and to those who know them among the noblest of birds, are vanishing everywhere. The griffons are like limping stragglers behind a defeated army, the few remaining lammergeiers have fled north to a last sanctuary in the Pyrenees, the black vulture has become so rare I saw it only twice above the Spanish mainland in the last five years I lived there.

The same grim catalogue – it could go on and on – could of course

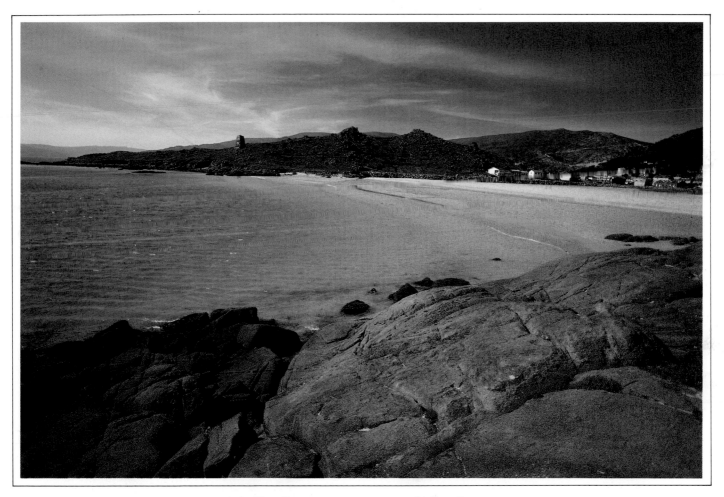

NEAR CARNOTA IN THE PROVINCE OF LA CORUÑA

be compiled for all the rest of Europe, and for most of the world too. As careless human pressure on the landscape grows, the living mantle that covers it becomes more and more torn and mutilated. In Spain's case one fragile difference sets it apart from most countries – certainly in Europe and possibly within a global context. As a human living space Spain is large and thinly-populated. In Britain, in contrast, every square mile of land has a population density fifty times as great. Then the inhabitants of the Spains are, by the world's standards, prosperous. In all the many kingdoms few of the castle-language speaking peoples die of starvation. Finally, the palace is built on ladders – and its towers, battlements, and terraces are raised higher still. However systematically the ploughs gouge out the earth along the land's vertical plains, they tend to falter when the ground rears upwards. Even the Spaniard's ability to carve out his swallows'-nest platforms above his pueblo fails at a certain level. Beyond that level and right up to the snowline, the living landscape continues to thrive undisturbed.

A small population in relation to the vast size of the country. Prosperity at least as measured against the food and goods of four-fifths of the earth. A household of mountains where the cycles of Spanish birth, maturing, and death take place without invading the attics above. Together they give Spain an extraordinary and heartwarming resilience. Olives and vines, maize and rice, have colonized the country. They have not subjugated the land – if anything they have enriched it. The royal roads, man-made as they may be, are a glory, a treasure-trove of ferns and flowers that might otherwise have been lost. Gypsies and the country-people burn the scrub but for every circle of land they clear, somewhere else – on some abandoned hillside, in some now-deserted ravine – the *mattoral* will be creeping in and refilling the puncture their ancestors made.

Brenan's wolves have gone from the Alpujarras, but they have not deserted the country altogether. A few packs still hunt Spain's higher, more remote mountains elsewhere. The mongooses, foxes, badgers, and genets, together with the Guadálmez's terrapins, may have been dispossessed in my valley, but climb back into the sierras above the Cabrito ridge, find another uncleared space of land behind another unplundered stream, and they will all be there. Lammergeiers still soar above the Pyrenees. If the griffon vultures that once circled the Gibraltar Straits in flocks have gone, head inland for the ravine-spanning city of

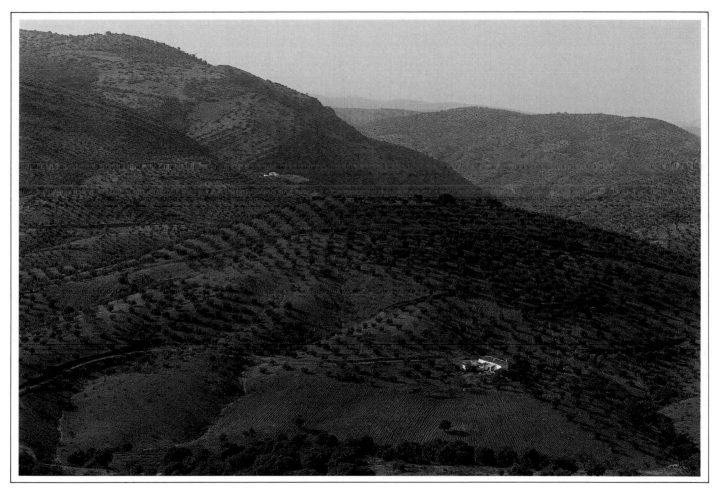

Near Alcalá la Real in the province of Jaén

Ronda — a few of them, at least, will be floating high above Ronda's hills. Perhaps somewhere an ebony-feathered black vulture will be circling among them. Even the Spanish lynx precariously remains. Walk out at night into the marshes of the Coto Doñana to the south of Seville, settle down, and wait for the dawn. In the first light it is still possible to catch the elegant leopard-like silhouette of the animal's head against the sky, and feel its feral presence among the reeds.

Man makes landscape, landscape makes man. In the African bush the most important daily ritual is the dawn inspection of the ground round a camp, to see from the tracks and droppings and trampled grass what the wild has been up to during the night. The animals will have gone with the darkness, but their spoor will still be there. In Spain, using a time-scale not of one night but centuries and the tracks of man in place of those of the animals, the landscape can be read like the African hunters read the bush. On the beaches of Spain's southern shores there grows a wild sea lily, *Pancratium illyricum*. The tall long-leaved plant with its scented white trumpets looks as if it has been there for ever, as natural a part of the coast as the rocks or waves. It has not. The ancient Phoenicians discovered its bulb was a hallucigen, and used it like alcohol or tobacco. Wherever their voyages took them and the local conditions were right, they planted it. The sea lily has increased its range on its own since then, but whenever the traveller finds it he can be fairly certain that somewhere close the Phoenicians landed and made a settlement thousands of years before him.

Inland the ox-blood red trunks of the cork oak forests, like the one which covered my valley, are among the most familiar sights of Andalucía. They too look like an immemorial part of the landscape. The trees indeed are — but not their appearance. In its natural state the cork oak's trunk is a gnarled grey-brown. Even earlier settlers than the Phoenicians discovered that the oak's bark, the cork, had remarkable properties. From then on the trees have been stripped every 7-9 years, the time it takes for the bark to grow back, and the cork crop has become one of the south's most valuable resources. Behind the forests and reaching far back to the rim of the Meseta are lonely meadows carpeted in spring for acre after acre with pink and gold bee-orchids. Their profusion too looks as natural as the sea lily or the red-trunked cork trees, but again it is not. Naturally the bee-orchid tends to grow only in tiny scattered clusters where conditions suit it exactly. Centuries

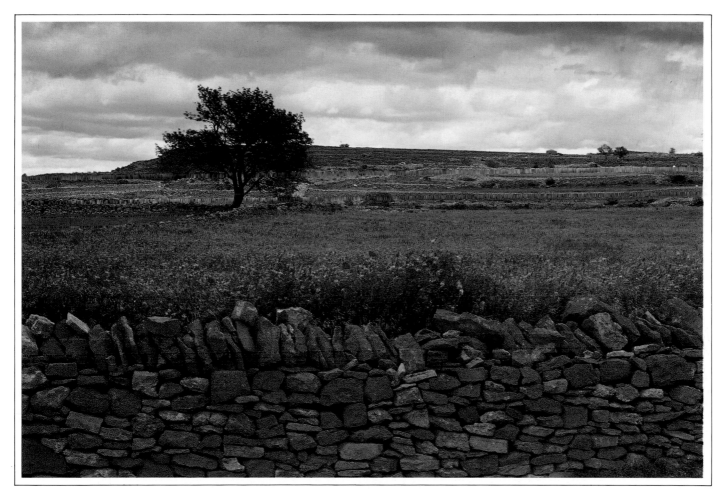

NEAR CANTAVIEJA IN THE PROVINCE OF TERUEL

of grazing by Andalusian sheep herds, which crop the competing grasses to a level that favours the orchid, have let the flower spread out over great swathes of land that under natural conditions would have been unavailable to it.

Sometimes, walking in unfamiliar parts of Spain, I have found myself in huge pastures that even in the lushness of the springtime countryside, seem particularly rich and ancient and undisturbed. There will be scented waist-high grass, drifts of scarlet poppies, larks and red-rumped swallows and hunting kestrels, deer and troops of wild boar. Silent and untouched by man, the pastures seem to be part of the

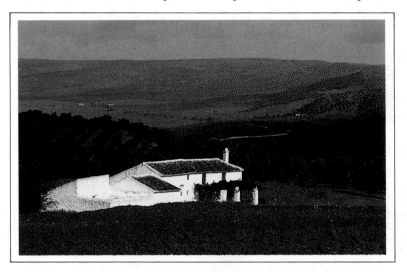

NEAR ALHAMA DE GRANADA IN THE PROVINCE OF GRANADA

old original landscape as it was before even the earliest Iberians arrived. In a sense they are just that and over the years I have learnt to be extremely wary of them. Almost always in such a place I will have wandered into the grazing grounds of fighting bulls. The Spanish fighting bull, for all its courage and ferocity, is not a wild animal at all. A result of early selective breeding, it is a man-made cross between the native cattle of Iberia and domesticated bulls brought in by the Carthaginians. For at least five hundred years, and probably much longer, its presence has kept large parts of Spain as they were long before Columbus sailed or the Armada put to sea. Ironically both the bull and its pastures, together with their communities of wildlife, would

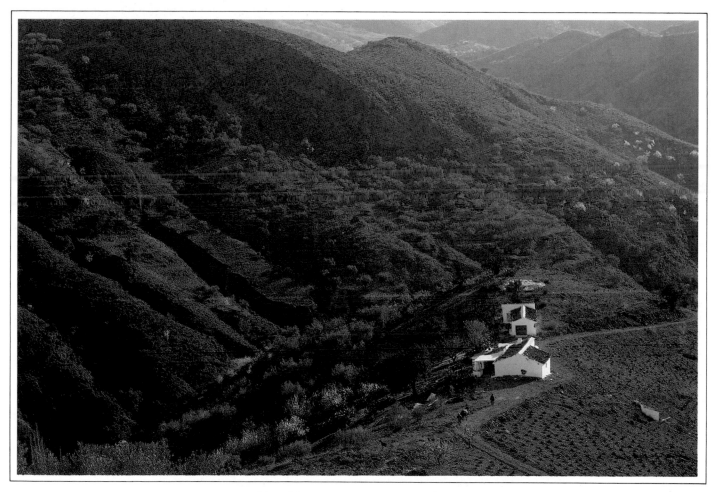

Near Cómpeta in the province of Málaga

be the first casualties if the threat to ban the *corrida* became a reality. The bull has no function outside the ring – other breeds produce beef more cheaply – and the pastures are ideally suited to being ploughed up for prairie farming. Meanwhile, another piece of man's spoor on the land, the *toro bravo* continues to act as a highly effective warden of the wilderness.

For the traveller with a perceptive eye it is possible to learn more about Spain from its landscape than any other country I know. The leavings of what has gone before – a sea lily, an almond tree in blossom, a mud-coated bull standing in the heat-haze of a summer plain – may have an immensely long pedigree, but they present themselves as freshly and vividly as the day they were first woven into the land. Today modern Spain is growing and changing more swiftly than anywhere else in Europe. Barcelona is becoming as chic as Paris, Seville is beginning to make San Francisco look dowdy, even Madrid, a city described by Henry Adams as at best a hole and in rainy weather a place fit only to drown rats in, is rapidly catching up on East Grinstead. Yet outside the cities, the kingdoms of the Spains still possess something that in the end owes nothing to man. A singular daemon haunts the palace whose Pyrennean walls, as the strutting *generalísimo* knew, shut Europe out. Or rather a clutch of daemons. The Spains are too diverse and distinct to harbour just one.

When I lived there and travelled the country, the daemons were so familiar I barely noticed them. Now away from Spain – and absence from much-loved places gives them a needle-sharp clarity in the mind's eye – images of their haunts return to me. Roncesvalles in spring, with the chestnut tree candles glowing up the sides of the winding pass, and the whole high land stretching beyond like the pegged-out hide of a Miura bull. The damp green valleys and ravines of Cataluña and the Basque country, where mist and rain are as constant companions as the fierce clear sun of the south. The ice and winds in winter, the searing heat in summer, and always the silence and desolation of the central plateau with the sentinel windmills standing guard above the lonely villages. On the west coast the rocky bays and little harbours from where the Basque whalers set out, on the east the bright green waters of the Mediterranean.

The pass of Despeñaperros that leads southwards from the hills into God's own garden and granary, Andalucía. The scent of orange blossom

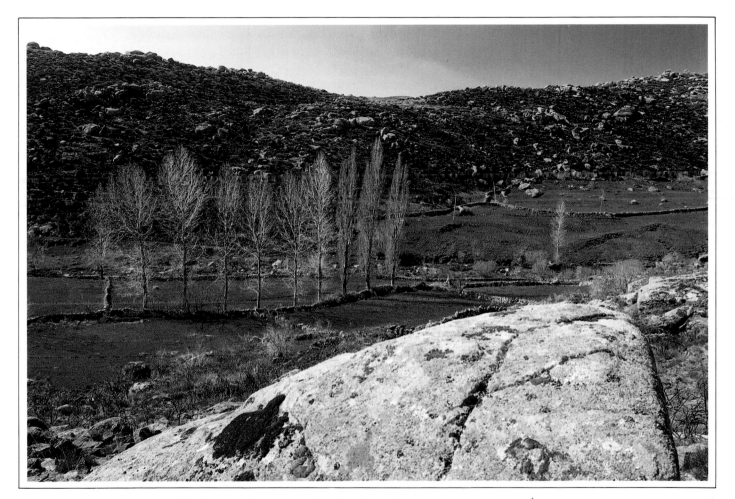

THE SIERRA DE GREDOS NEAR SAN MARTÍN DEL PIMPOLAR IN THE PROVINCE OF ÁVILA

outside Seville. A crescent moon rising above Granada and the snow-flanks of the Sierra Nevada beyond. The rolling dunes and sandy wastelands beyond Almería. The secret hidden villages of the high sierras: Grazalema mortared like a martlet's nest to the rocks; Ubrique, the leather-working pueblo, its alleys filled with the stench of drying hide and a rainbow's end resting on its roofs; Ronda, straddling the river's gorge with thick winter snow covering the old bullring and ravens wheeling over the frozen pools far below. Skeins of flamingoes in the dusk above Seville's minarets and palm trees, and Carmona, the frying-pan of Spain, in August when the heat is so fierce the cobbles flake and crack. The translucent spring-green of the slender poplars; the nightingales singing in the courtyards of the Alhambra; the clouds of whistling green and bronze bee-eaters announcing the turning year; the white sands west of Tarifa where only gulls and porpoises keep company with the waves.

Every last small corner – and there are thousands more in all the kingdoms – has its own particular spirit. None of them would admit to anything in common: even if they did their tenants, the peoples of the Spains, would vigorously deny it. Yet I believe the kingdoms do share something. It is something surprisingly modest. Not passion or heat or drama, or any of the received wisdom about the Spanish character and landscape. Instead a mutual sense of purpose and sense of scale. In Spain man belongs to the land just as much as the land belongs to man. The two leave space between each other. They respect each other's privacy. If Spain is lonely, it is because both sides have agreed that is the right and proper condition for a working relationship between them.

I have the deepest respect for the relationship. Every year it allows the eagles to fly in over the valley, and across the towers and gardens of the palace that lies south of the Pyrenees.

Michael Busselle's photographs of the landscapes of the Spains are rare – and perhaps rarest of all because, for once, a photographer's work needs no comment or embroidery. His images of the Iberian countryside stand alone in their own right, as clear and austere and vital as the land itself. They answer for themselves and for Spain.

They are all that even the troublesome daemons of the kingdoms could ask.

Nicholas Luard

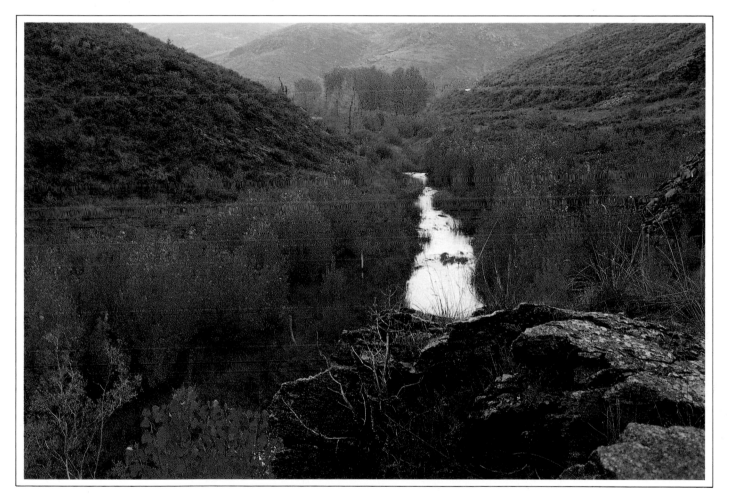

Near Naharros in the province of Guadalajara

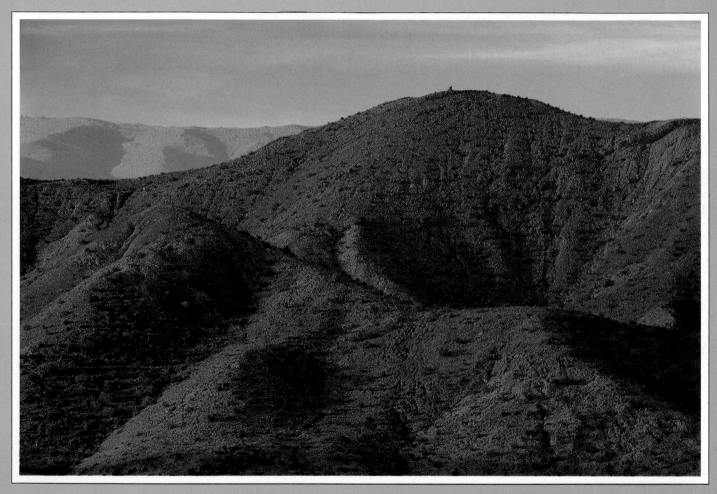

THE REGION KNOWN AS MINI HOLLYWOOD NEAR TABERNAS IN THE PROVINCE OF ALMERÍA

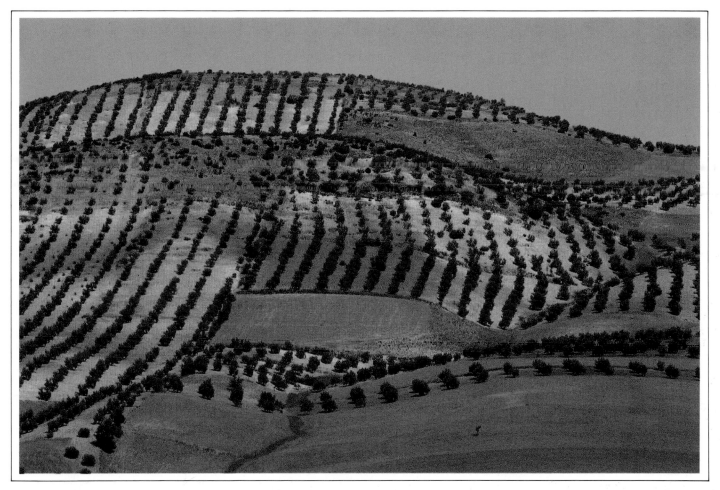

NEAR BAILÉN IN THE PROVINCE OF JAÉN

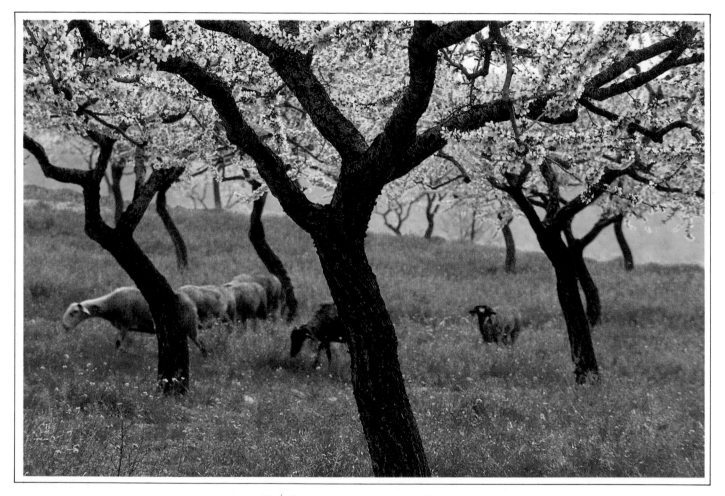

NEAR GANDESA IN THE PROVINCE OF TERUEL

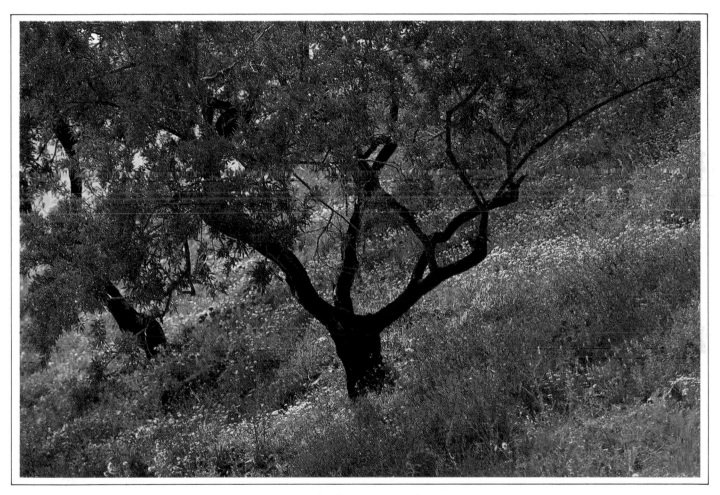

NEAR LENTEJÍ IN THE PROVINCE OF GRANADA

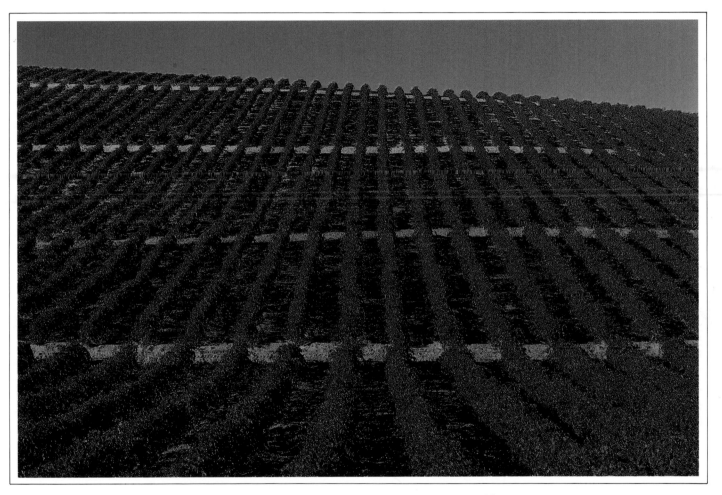

VINEYARDS NEAR JEREZ DE LA FRONTERA IN THE PROVINCE OF CÁDIZ

61

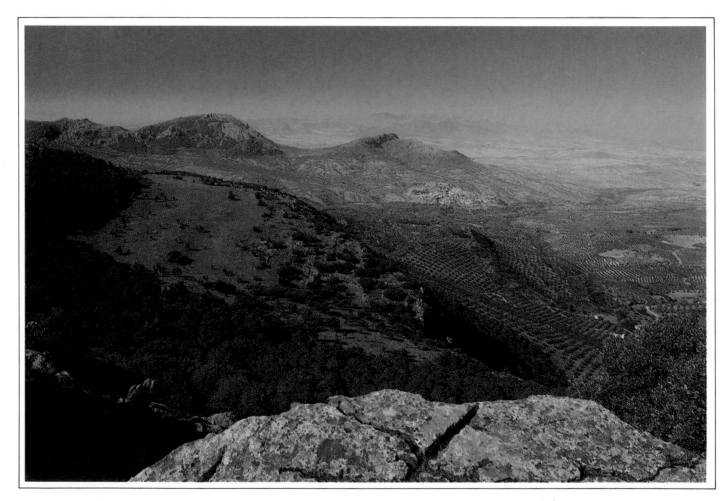

THE VIEW TOWARDS QUESADA FROM THE SIERRA DE CAZORLA IN THE PROVINCE OF JAÉN

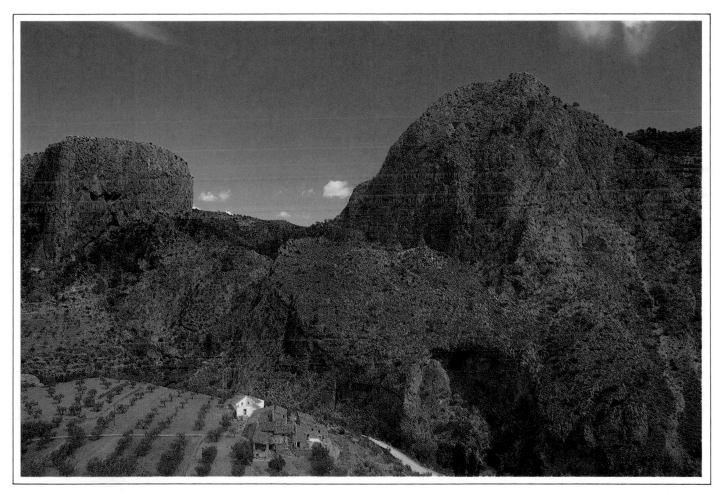

The Sierra de Alcaraz near Ayna in the province of Albacete

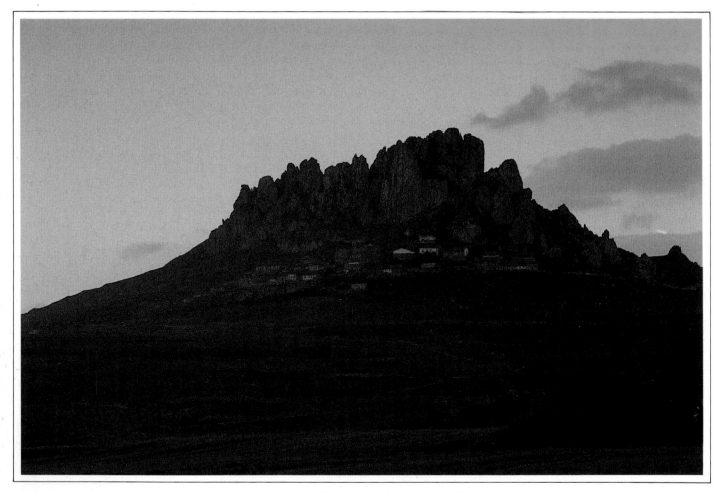

CELLORIGO NEAR HARO IN THE PROVINCE OF LA RIOJA

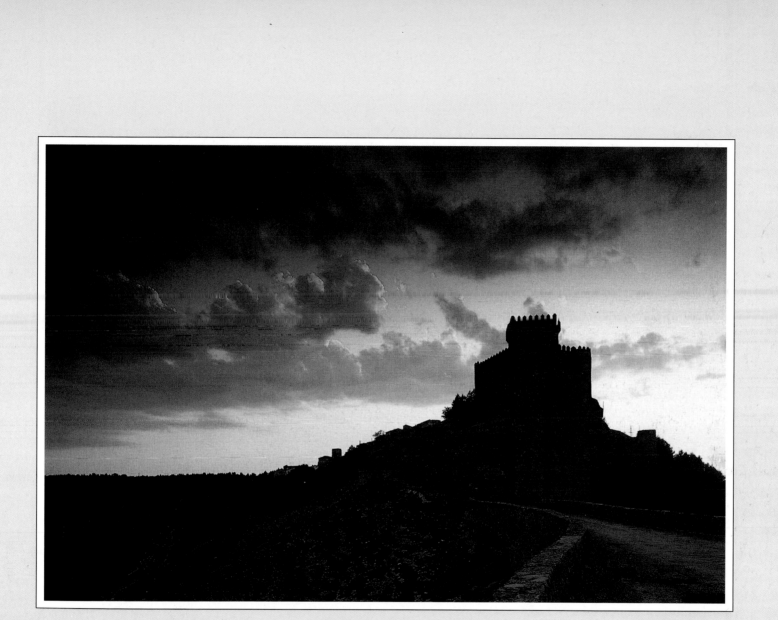

THE CASTLE OF ALARCÓN IN THE PROVINCE OF CUENCA

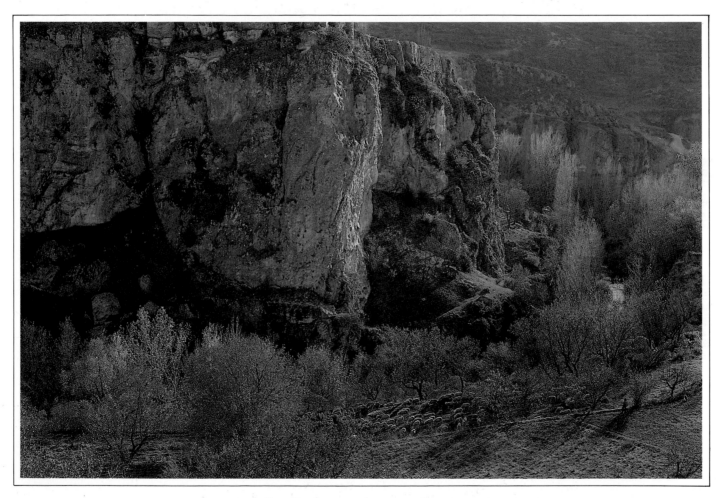

NEAR PRIEGO IN THE PROVINCE OF CUENCA

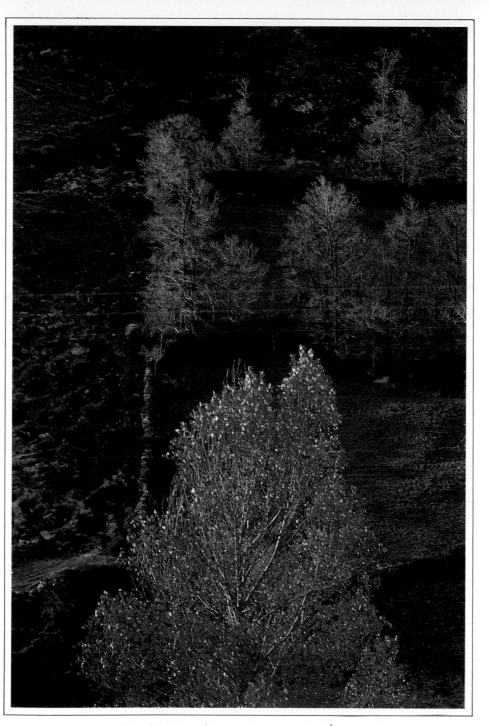

Near Hoyos del Espino in the province of Ávila

NEAR SAN PEDRO DE LA NAVE IN THE PROVINCE OF ZAMORA

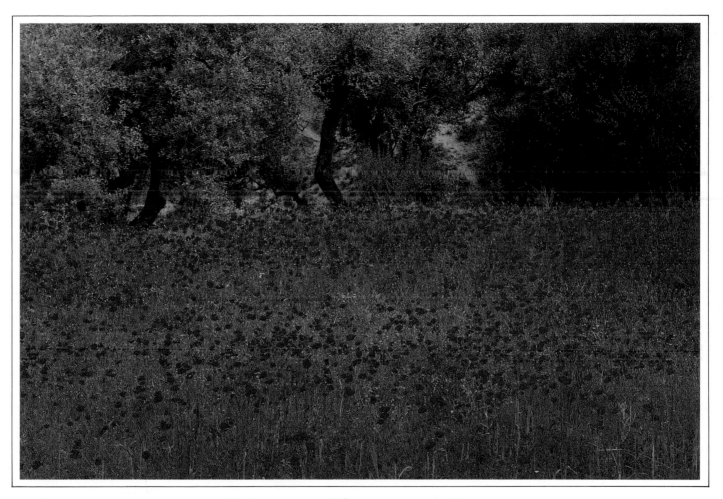

THE ALPUJARRAS NEAR UGÍJAR IN THE PROVINCE OF GRANADA

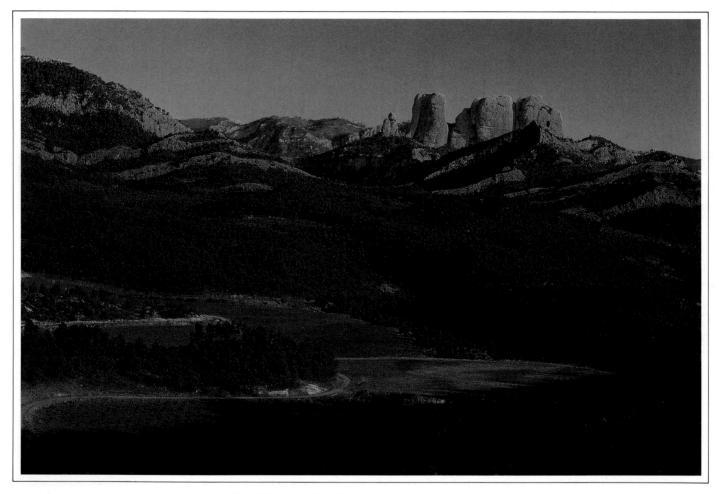

NEAR HORTA DE SANT-JUAN IN THE PROVINCE OF TERUEL

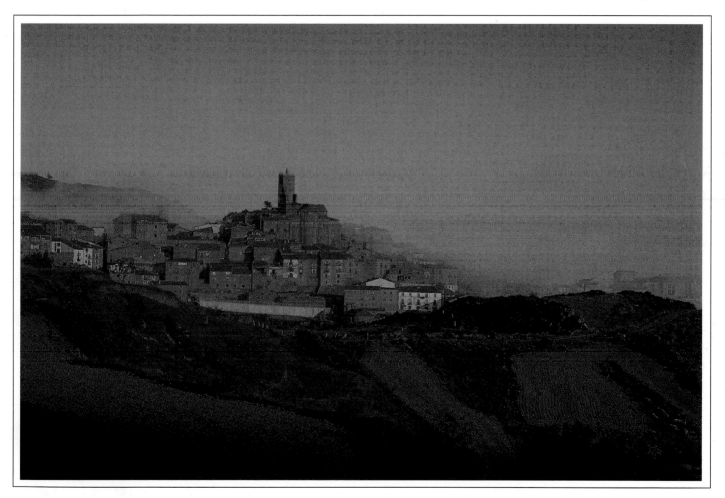

SOS DEL REY CATÓLICO IN THE PROVINCE OF ZARAGOZA

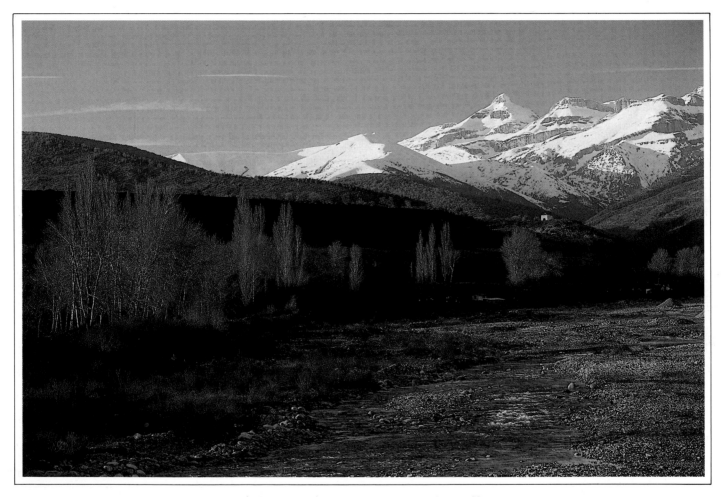

The Río Gallego near Sabinanigo in the province of Huesca

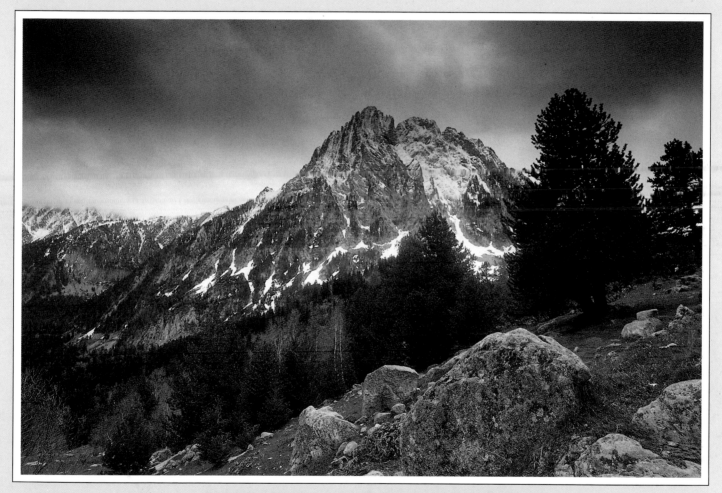

THE SIERRA DEL ENCANTATS IN THE NATIONAL PARK OF AIGUES TORTES
NEAR ESPOT IN THE PROVINCE OF LERIDA

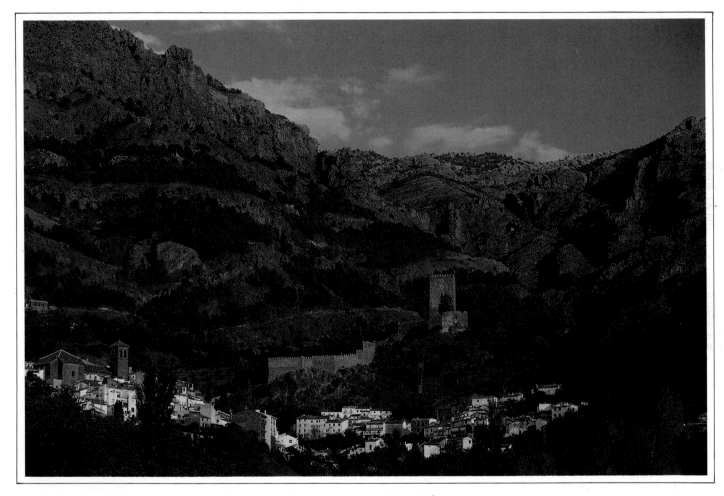

CAZORLA IN THE PROVINCE OF JAÉN

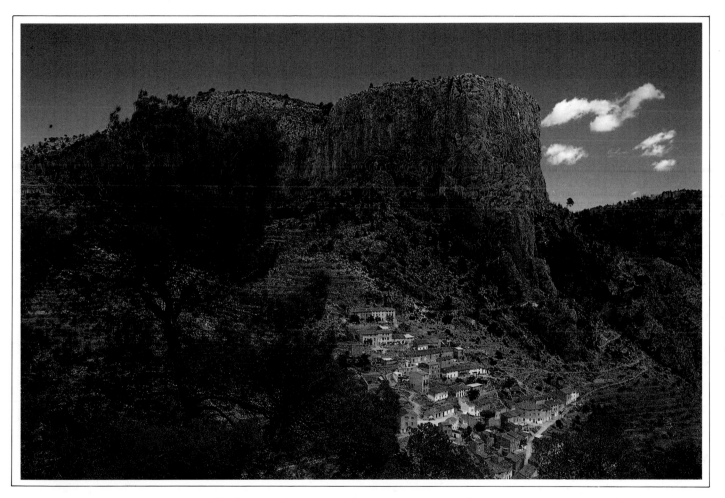

THE SIERRA DE ALCARAZ NEAR AYNA IN THE PROVINCE OF ALBACETE

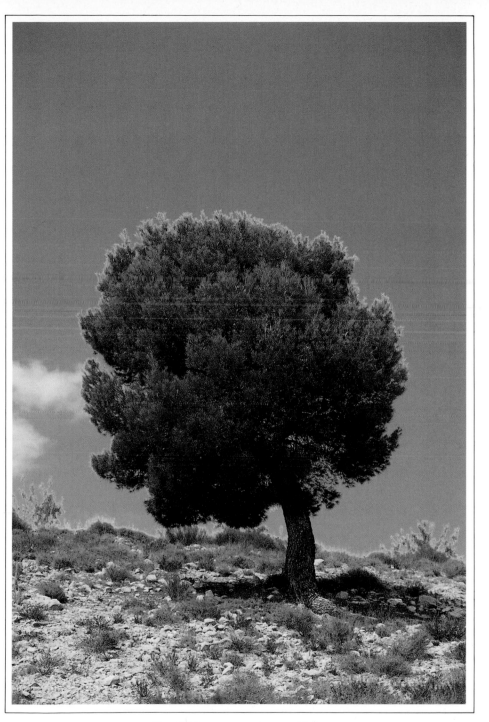

Near Tíscar in the province of Jaén

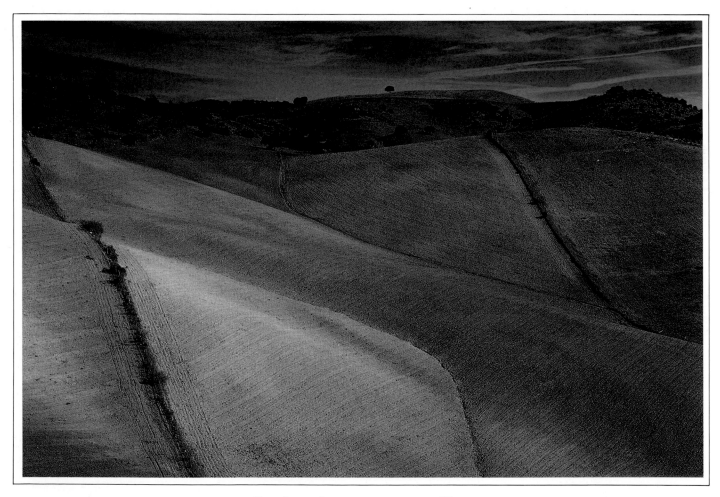

Near Algodoñales in the province of Cádiz

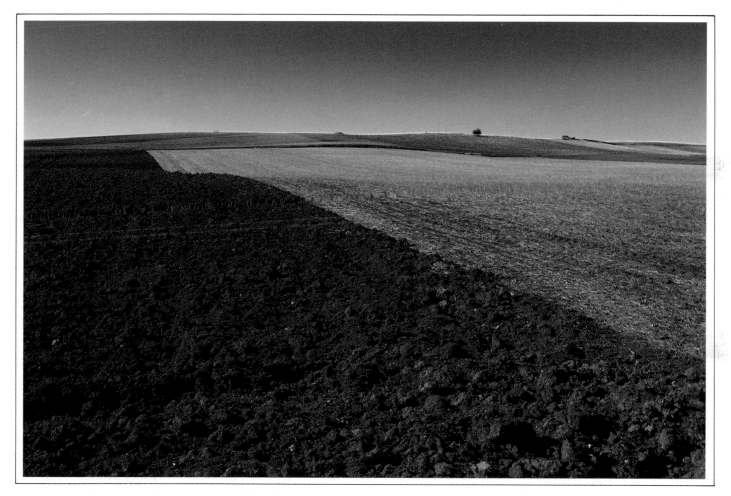

Near Mota del Cuervo in the province of Cuenca

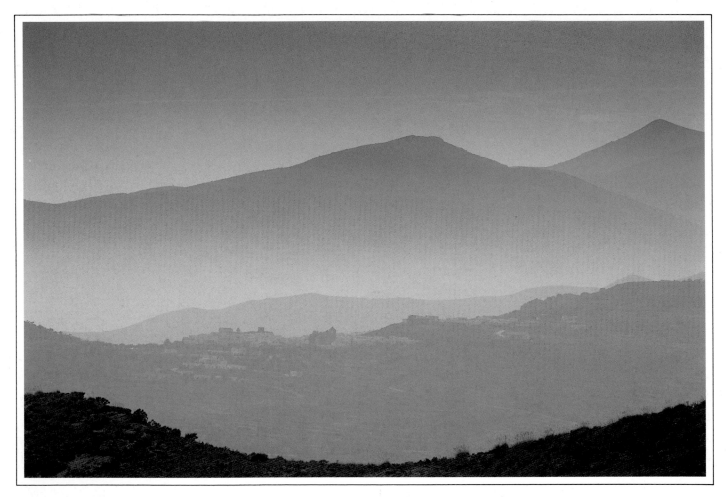

THE SIERRA DE GÁDOR NEAR FÉLIX IN THE PROVINCE OF ALMERÍA

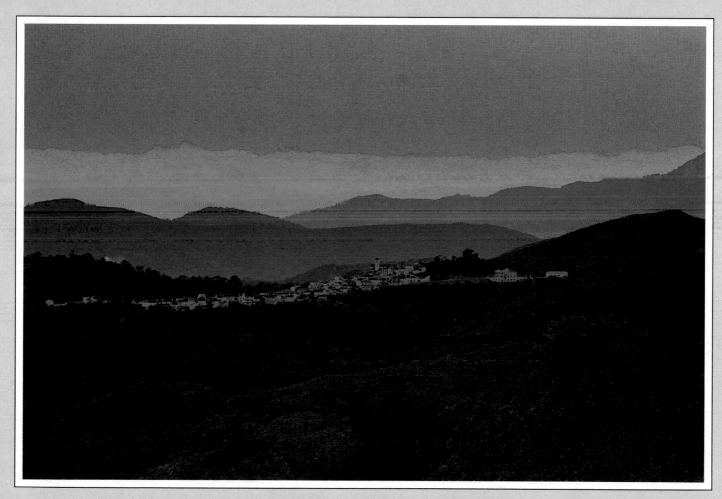

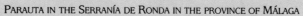

PARAUTA IN THE SERRANÍA DE RONDA IN THE PROVINCE OF MÁLAGA

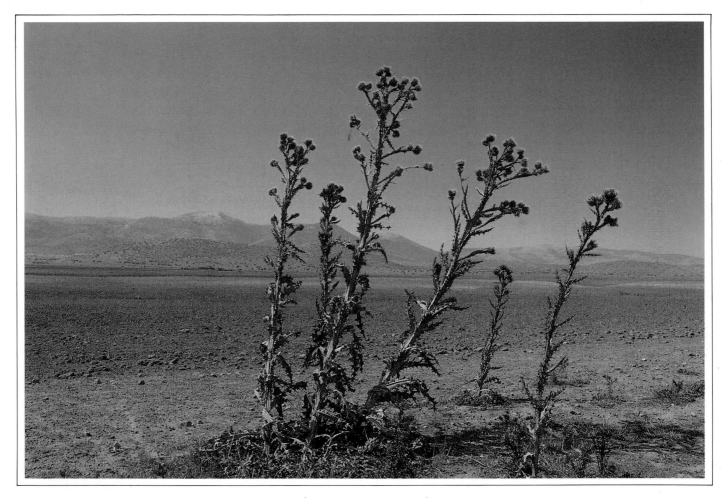

Near Huéscar in the province of Granada

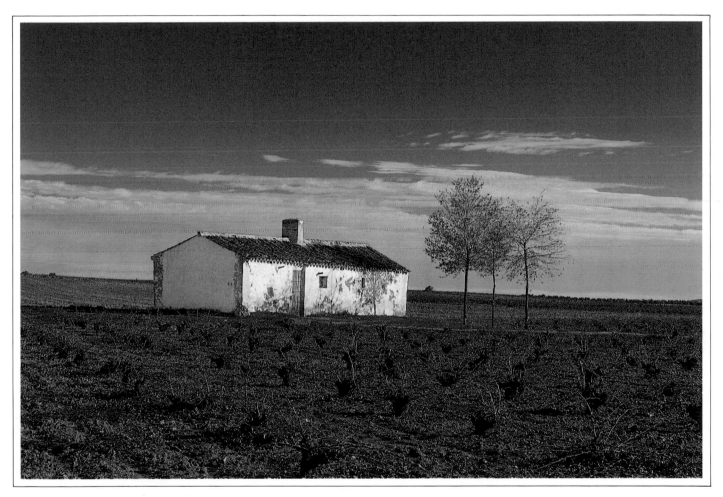

NEAR CAMPO DE CRÍPTANA IN THE PROVINCE OF CIUDAD REAL

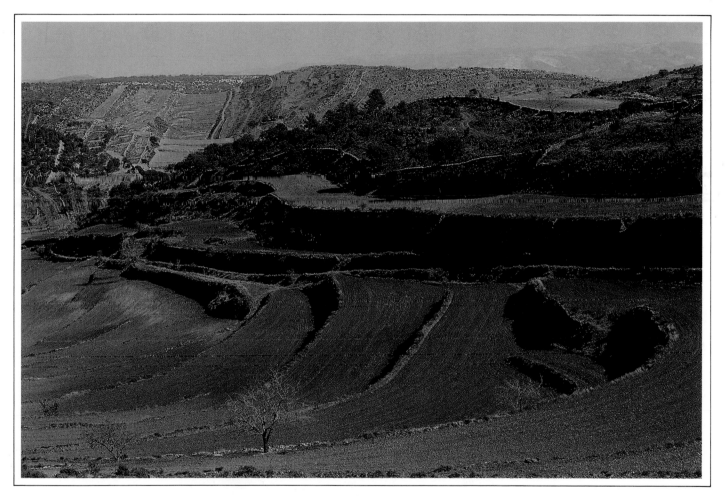

NEAR CAÑADA DE BENATANDUZ IN THE PROVINCE OF TERUEL

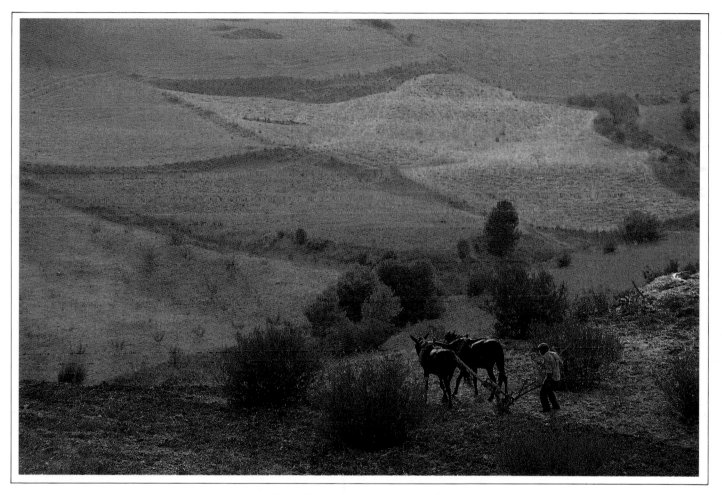

NEAR TÍSCAR IN THE PROVINCE OF JAÉN

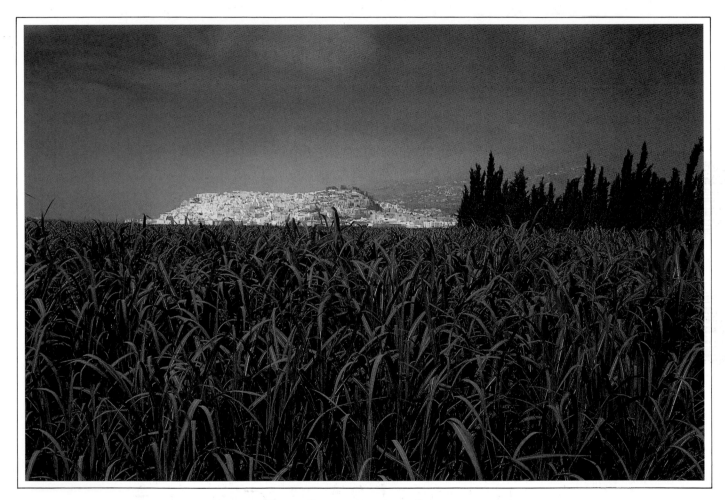

SALOBREÑA IN THE PROVINCE OF GRANADA

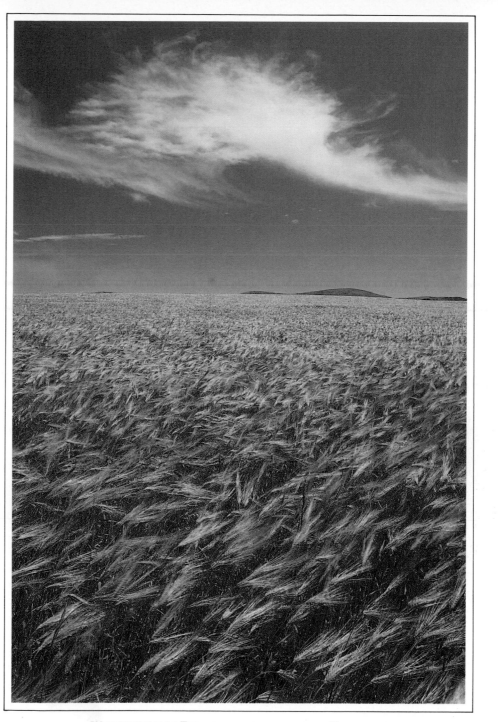

WHEATFIELDS NEAR TORDESILLAS IN THE PROVINCE OF VALLADOLID

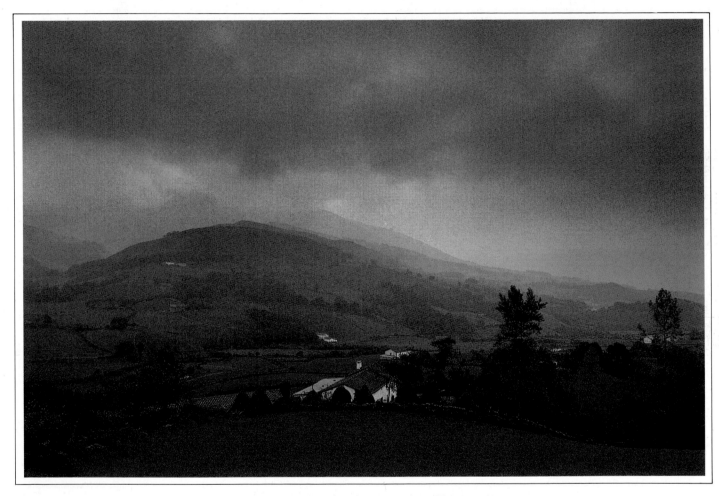

The Valle de Baztán in the province of Navarra

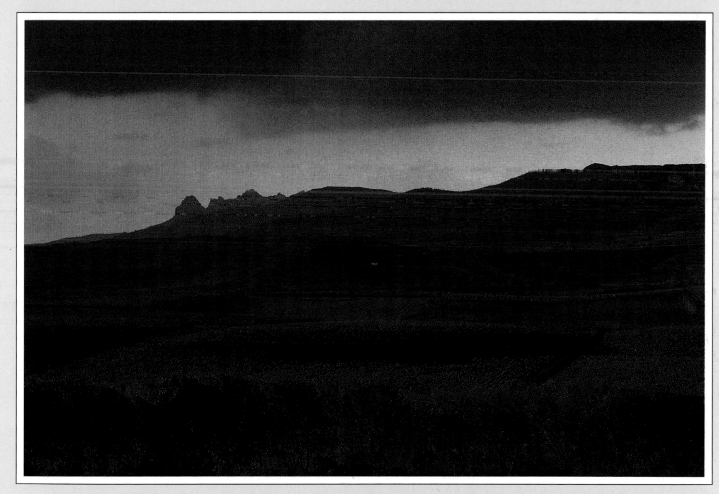

VINEYARDS NEAR BRIÑAS IN THE PROVINCE OF LA RIOJA

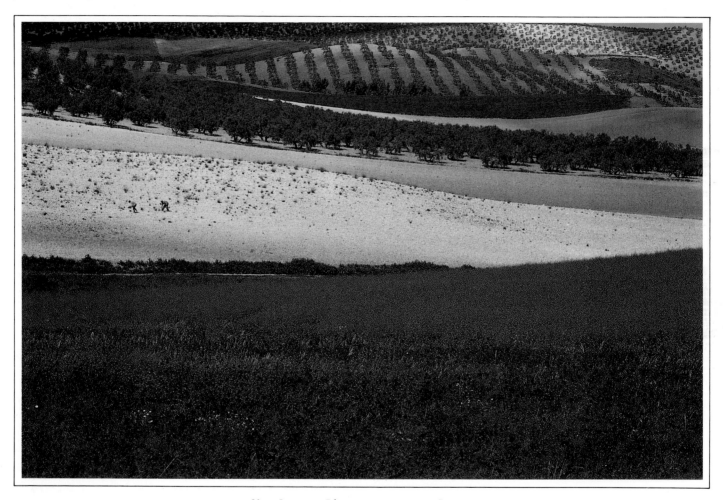

Near Lora del Río in the province of Sevilla

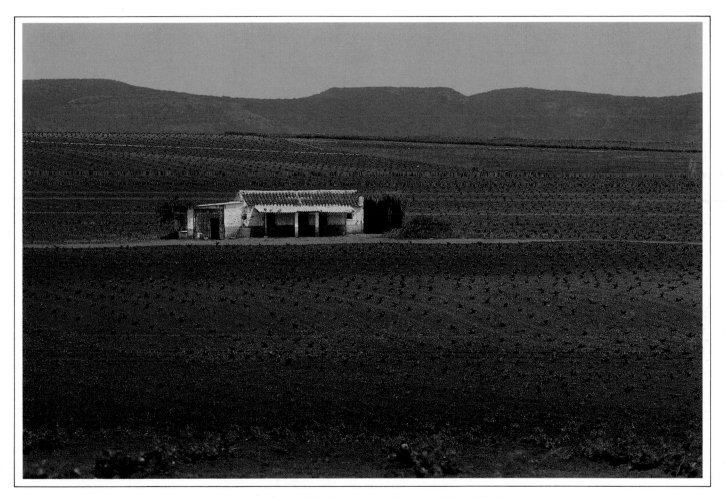

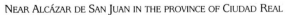
Near Alcázar de San Juan in the province of Ciudad Real

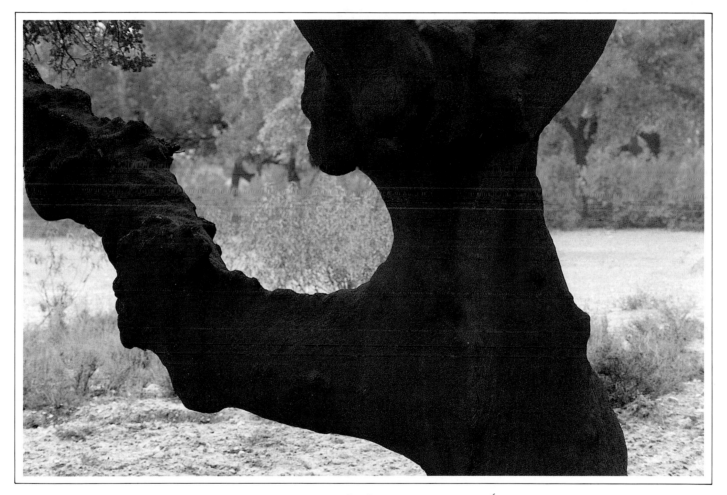

A CORK OAK NEAR ARENAS DE SAN PEDRO IN THE PROVINCE OF ÁVILA

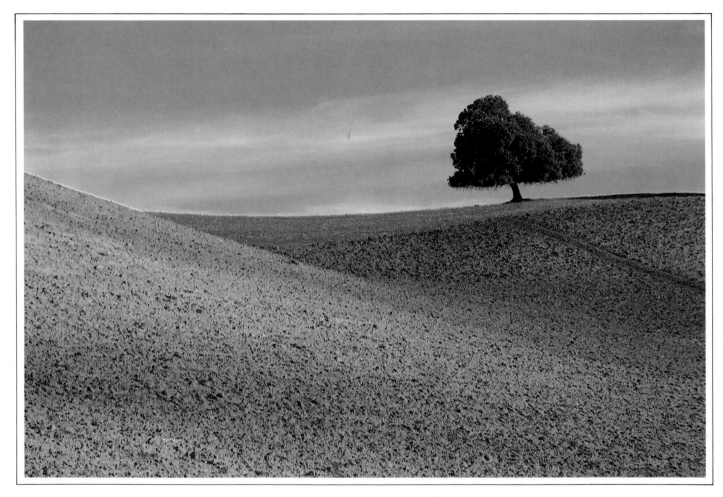

Near Ronda in the province of Málaga

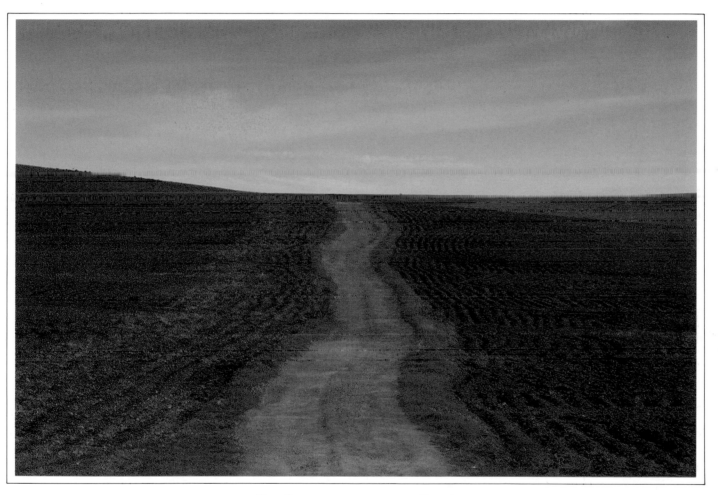

NEAR CARMONA IN THE PROVINCE OF SEVILLA

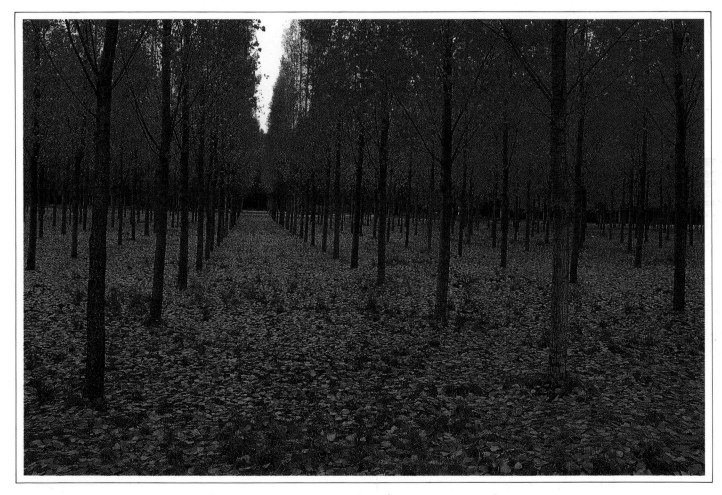

A plantation of poplars near Almazán in the province of Soria

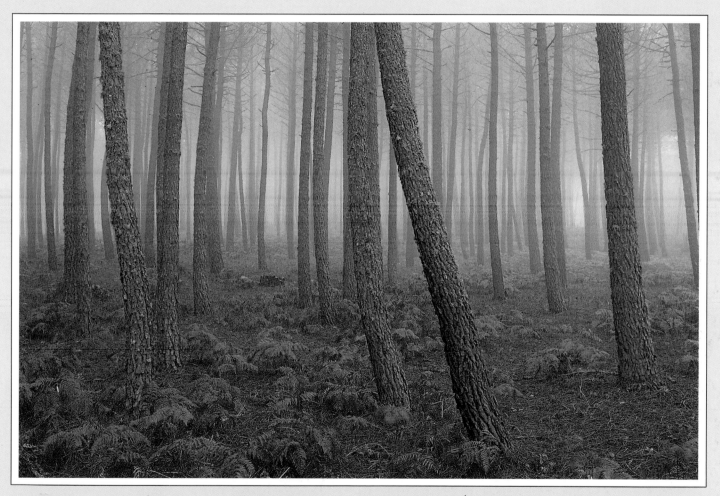

Near Arenas de San Pedro in the province of Ávila

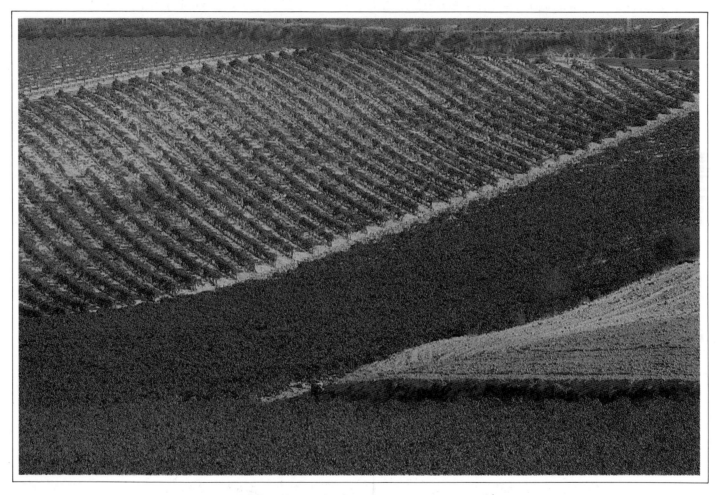

VINEYARDS NEAR JEREZ DE LA FRONTERA IN THE PROVINCE OF CÁDIZ

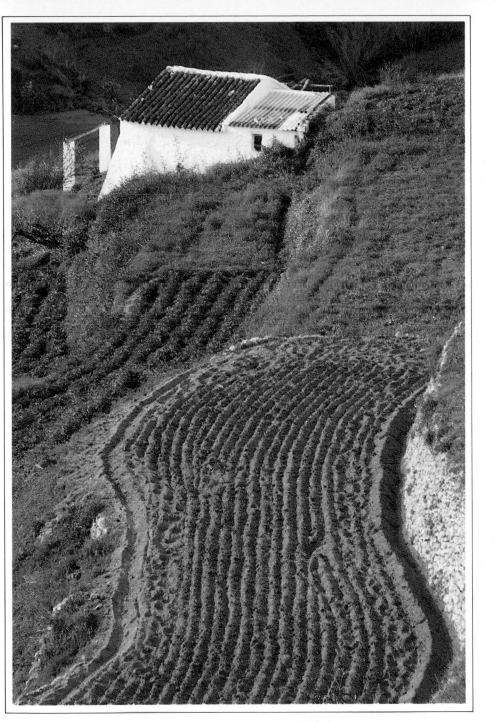

NEAR FRIGILIANA IN THE PROVINCE OF MÁLAGA

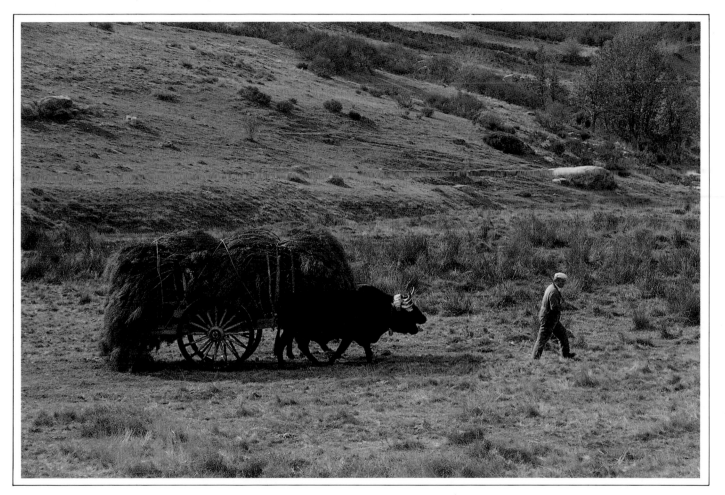

NEAR HOYOS DEL ESPINO IN THE PROVINCE OF ÁVILA

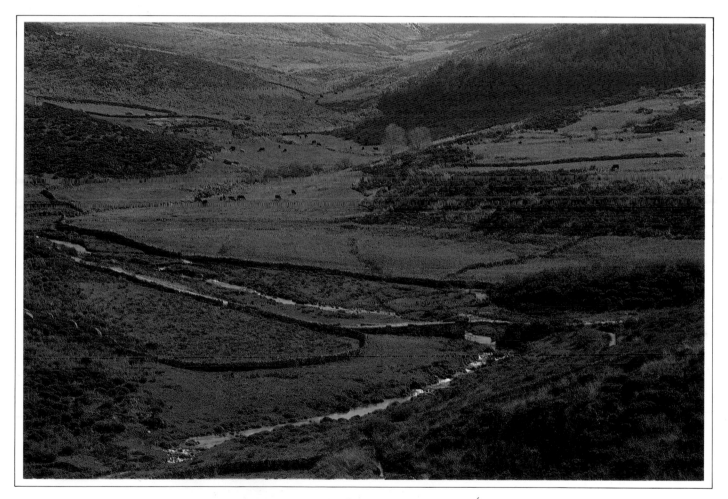

NEAR NAVARREDONDA DE GREDOS IN THE PROVINCE OF ÁVILA

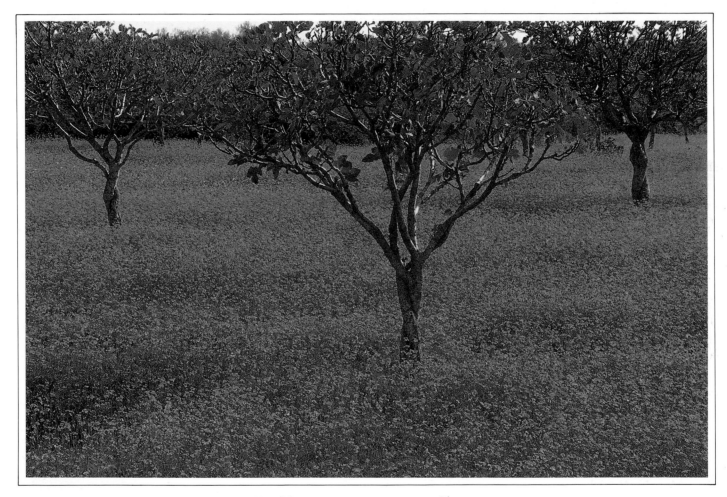

Near Montanchez in the province of Cáceres

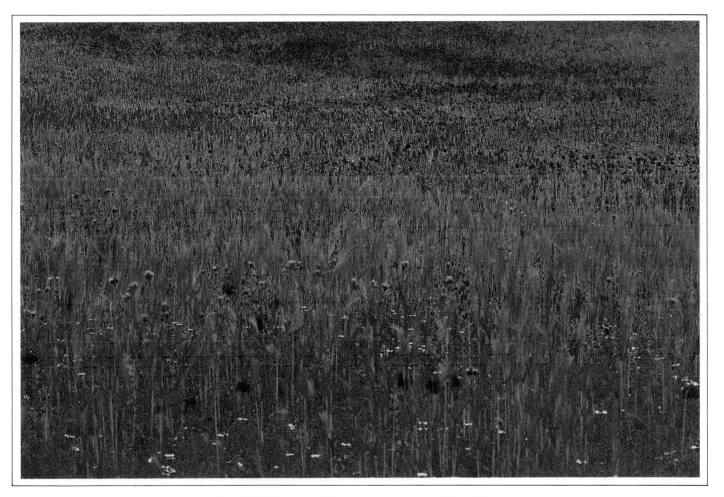

Near San Carlos del Valle in the province of Ciudad Real

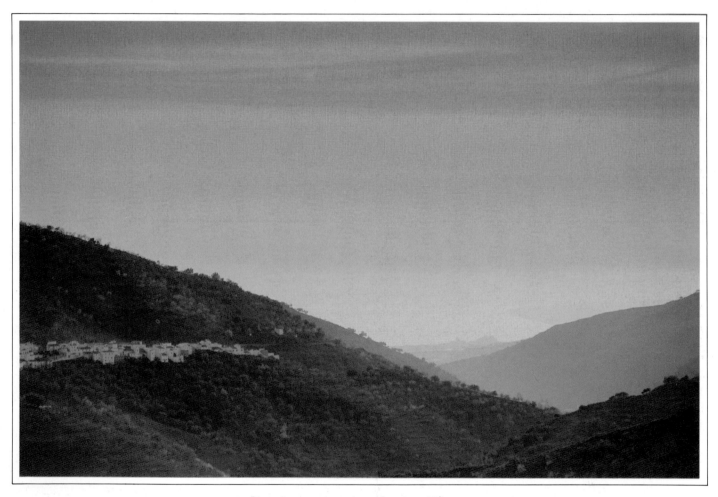

Near Algarrobo in the province of Málaga

THE VIEW FROM THE CASTLE OF ATIENZA IN THE PROVINCE OF GUADALAJARA

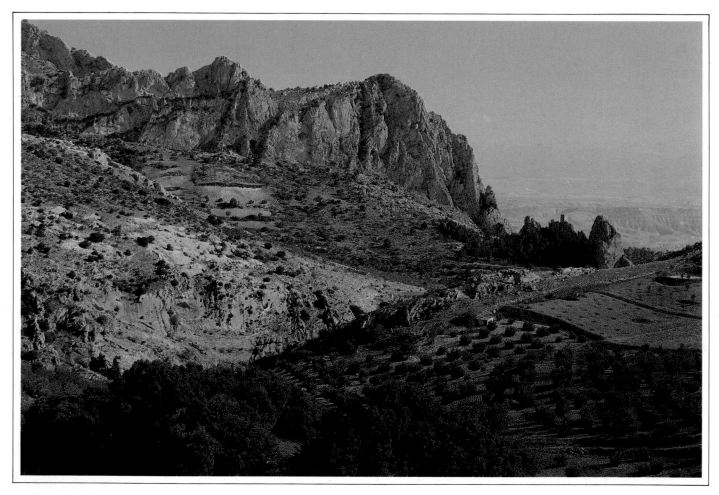

TÍSCAR IN THE PROVINCE OF JAÉN

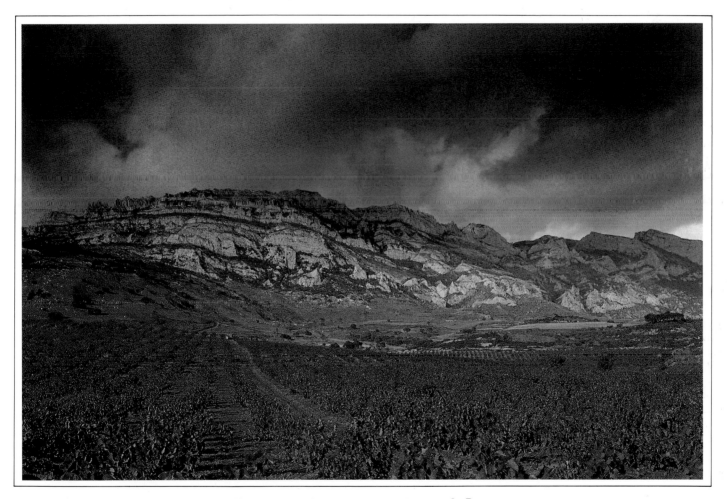

VINEYARDS NEAR LABASTIDA IN THE PROVINCE OF LA RIOJA

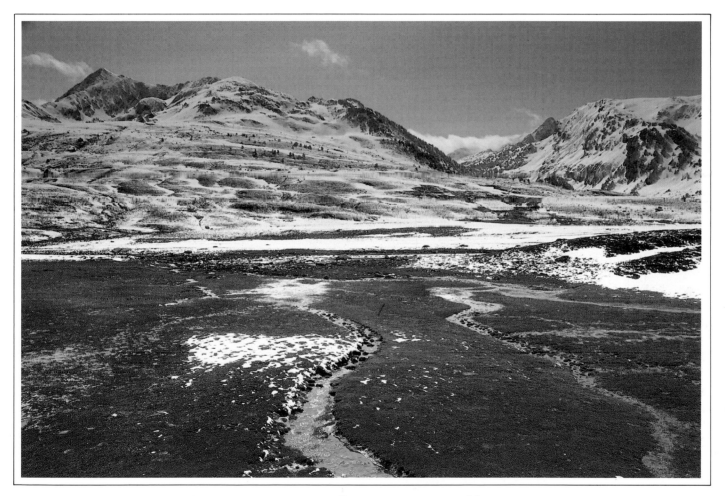

THE PLA DE BERET NEAR TREDOS IN THE PROVINCE OF LÉRIDA

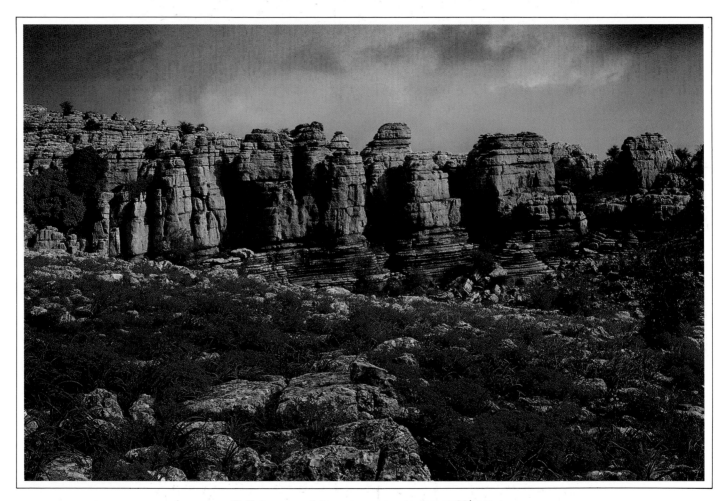

El Torcal near Antequera in the province of Málaga

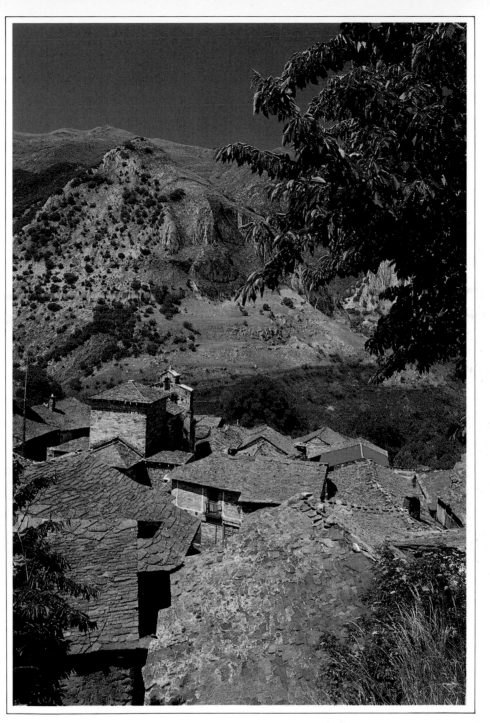

117

PEÑALBA DE SANTIAGO IN THE PROVINCE OF LEÓN

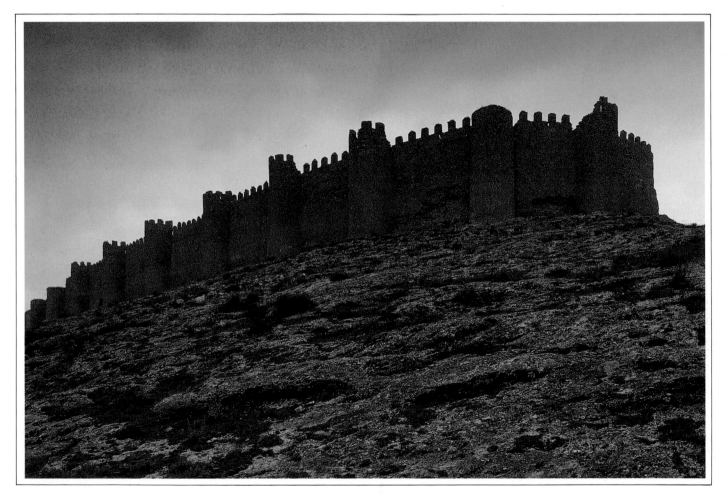

The castle of Berlanga de Duero in the province of Soria

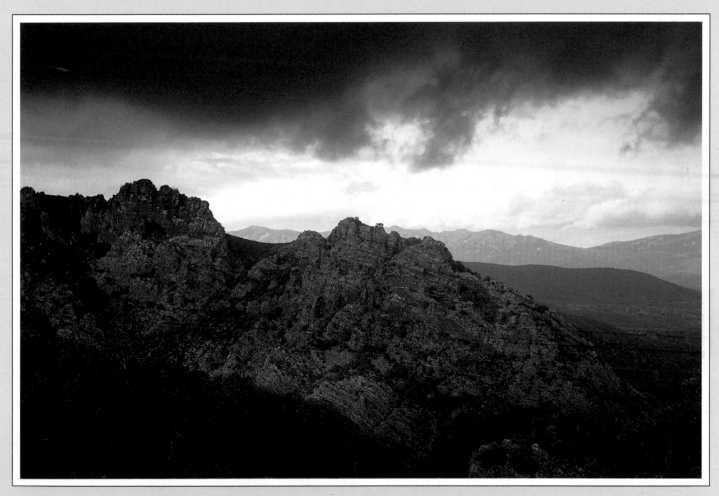

THE PUERTO DE SAN VICENTE NEAR GUADALUPE IN THE PROVINCE OF CÁCERES

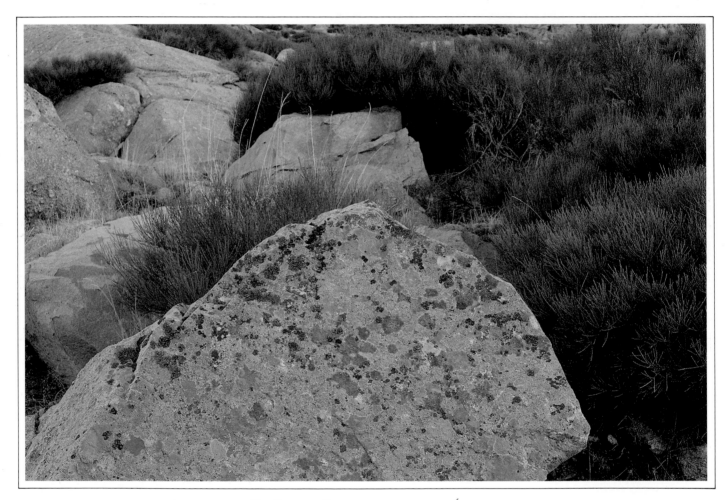

THE SIERRA DE GREDOS IN THE PROVINCE OF ÁVILA

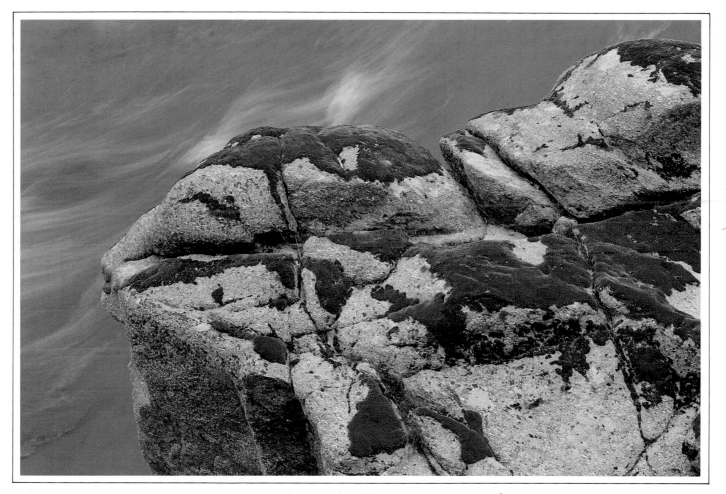

The Río Tiétar near Arenas de San Pedro in the province of Ávila

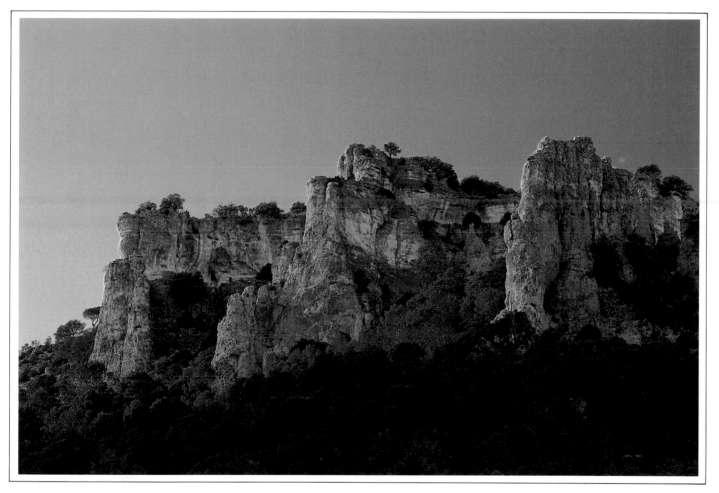

NEAR PRIEGO IN THE PROVINCE OF CUENCA

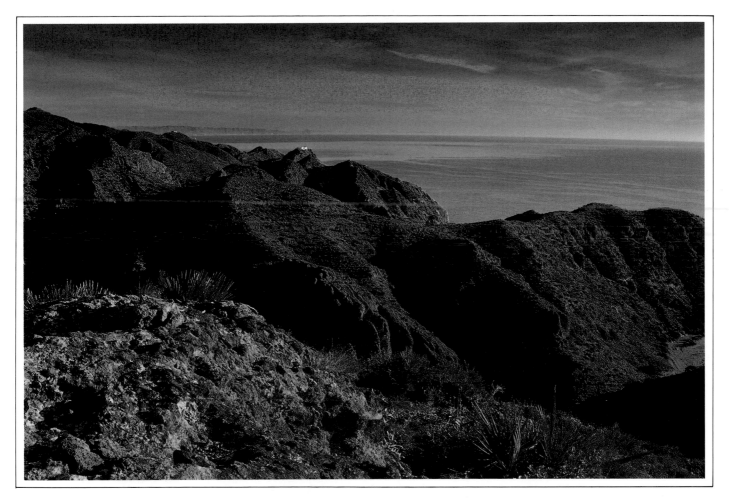

Near Carboneras in the province of Almería

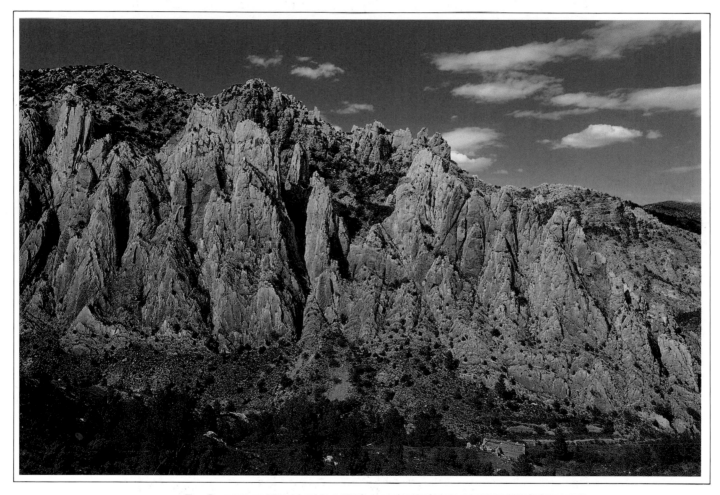

THE ORGANOS DE MONTORO NEAR VILLARLUENGO IN THE PROVINCE OF TERUEL

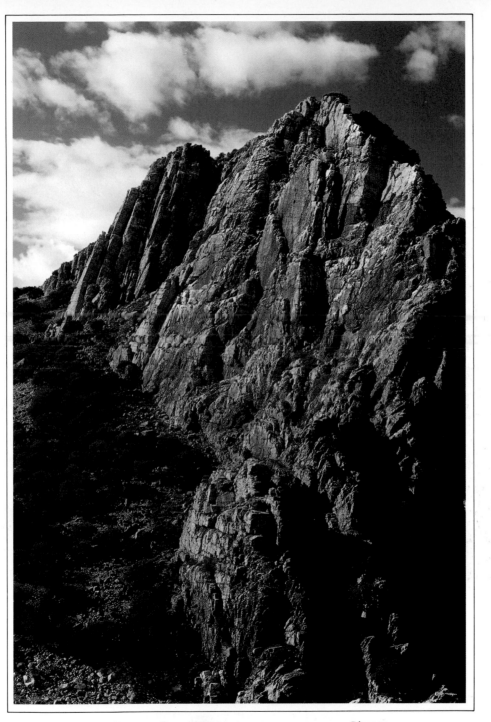

THE NATIONAL PARK OF MONFRAGUE IN THE PROVINCE OF CÁCERES

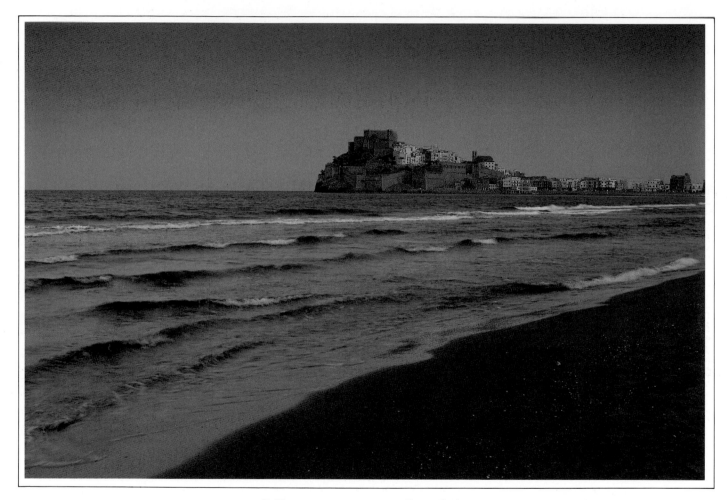

Peñíscola in the province of Castile-León

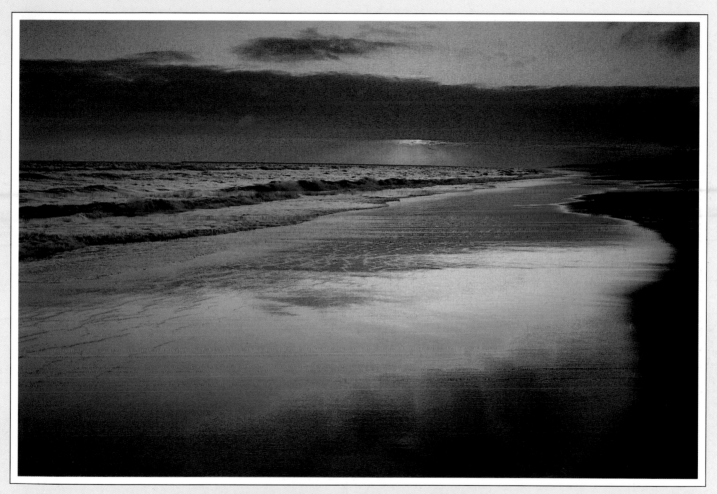

THE BEACH NEAR MAZAGON IN THE PROVINCE OF HUELVA

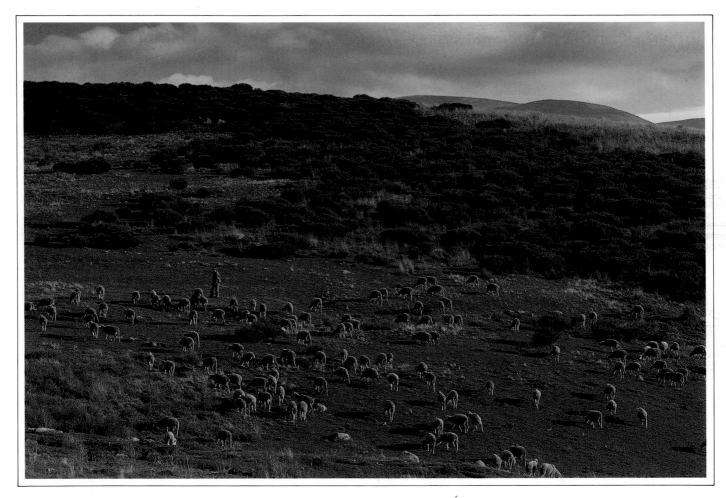

THE SIERRA DE GREDOS IN THE PROVINCE OF ÁVILA

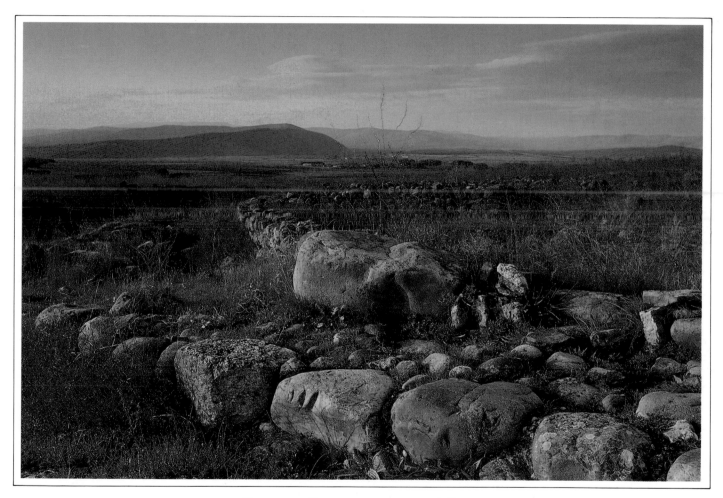

THE RUINS OF NUMANCIA IN THE PROVINCE OF SORIA

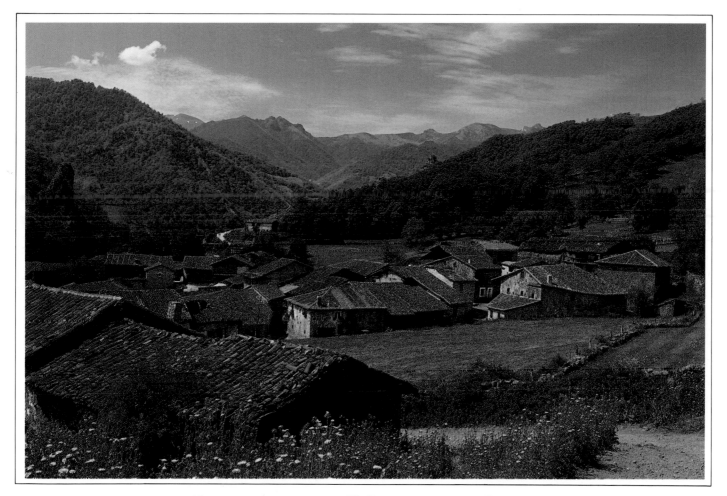

Mogrovejo in the valley of the Río Deva in the province of Cantabria

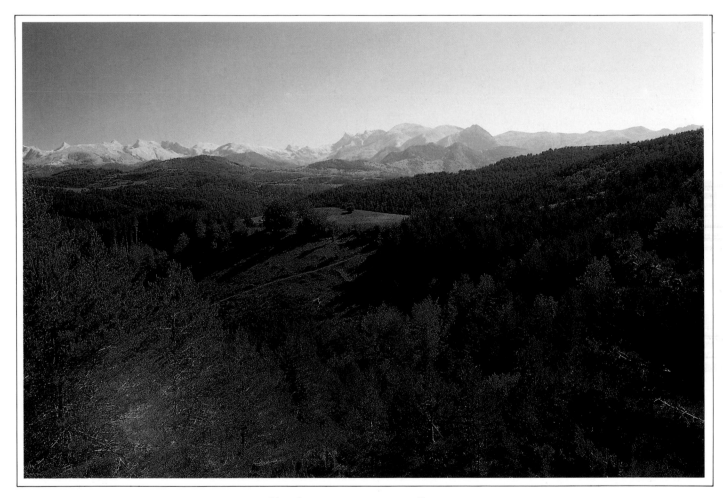

Near Isaba in the province of Navarra

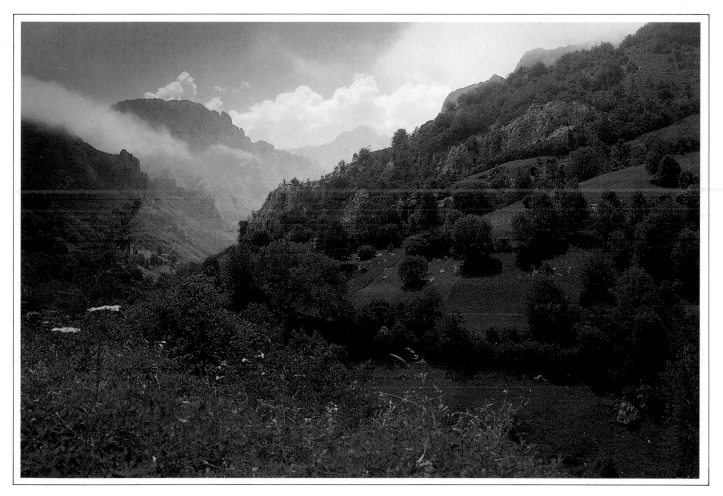

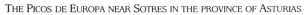

THE PICOS DE EUROPA NEAR SOTRES IN THE PROVINCE OF ASTURIAS

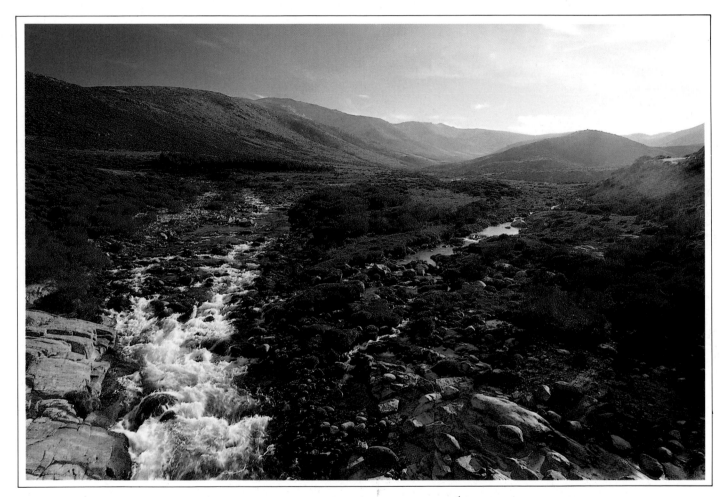

Near Hoyos del Espino in the Province of Ávila

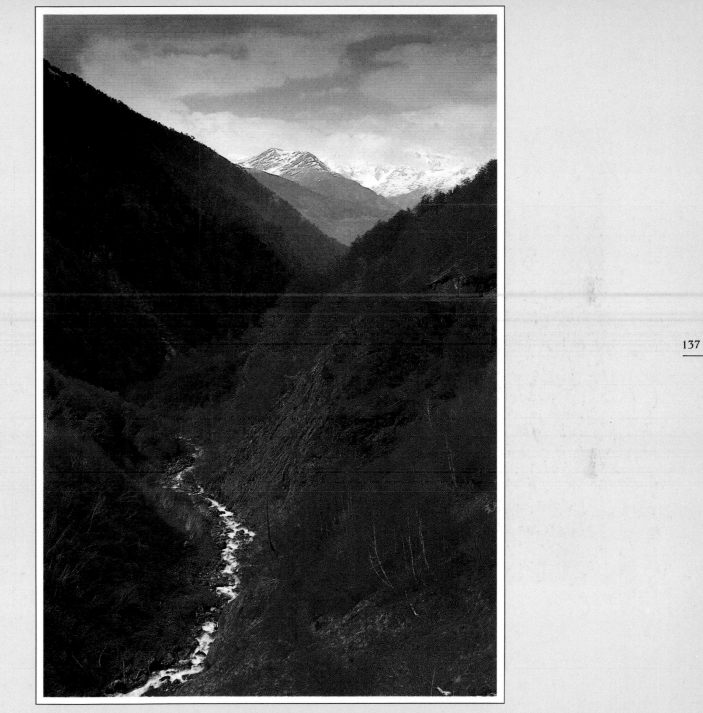

THE VALLEY OF THE RÍO VARRADOS NEAR VIELLA IN THE PROVINCE OF LÉRIDA

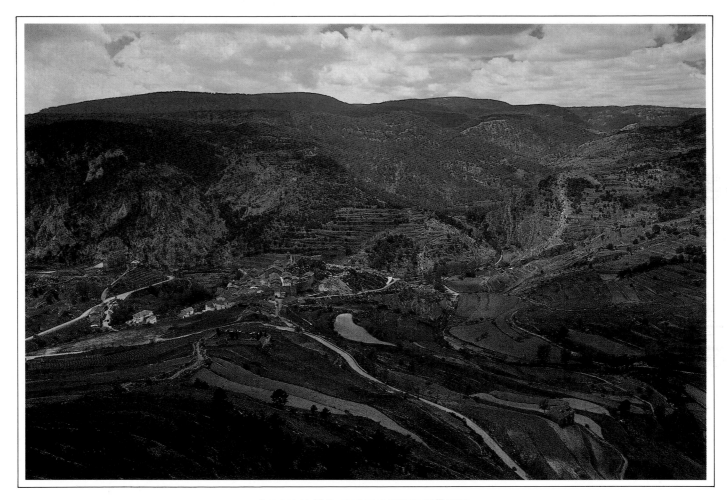

LINARES DE MORA IN THE PROVINCE OF TERUEL

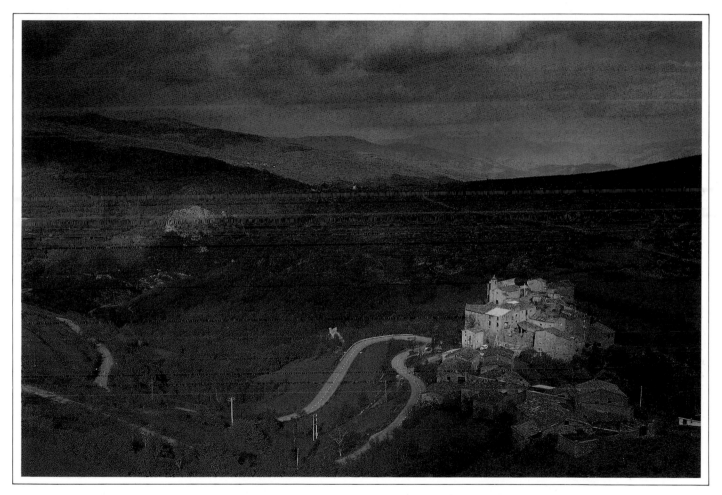

Near Pont de Suert in the province of Lérida

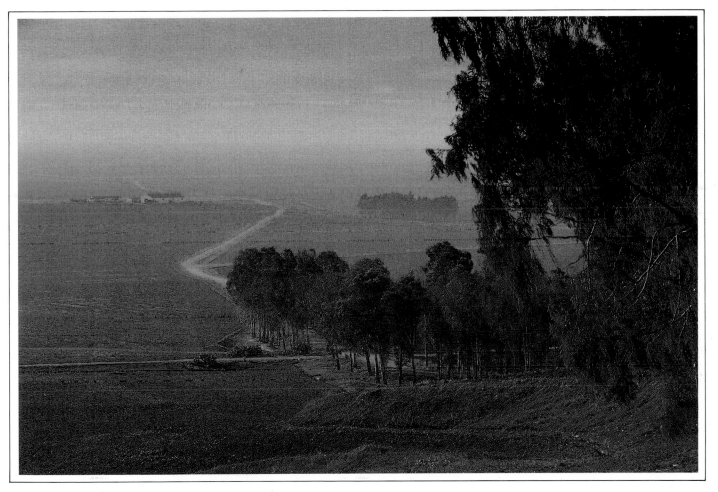

Near Carmona in the province of Sevilla

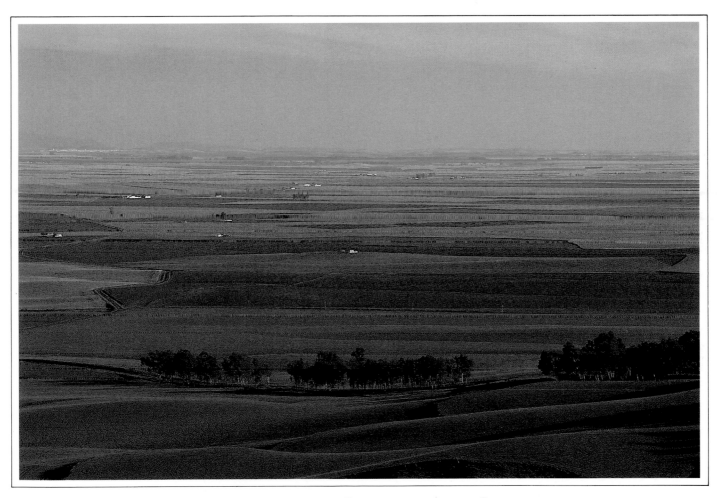

THE VIEW FROM THE WALLS OF CARMONA IN THE PROVINCE OF SEVILLA

NEAR VILLACARILLO IN THE PROVINCE OF JAÉN

NEAR VILLALPANDO IN THE PROVINCE OF ZAMORA

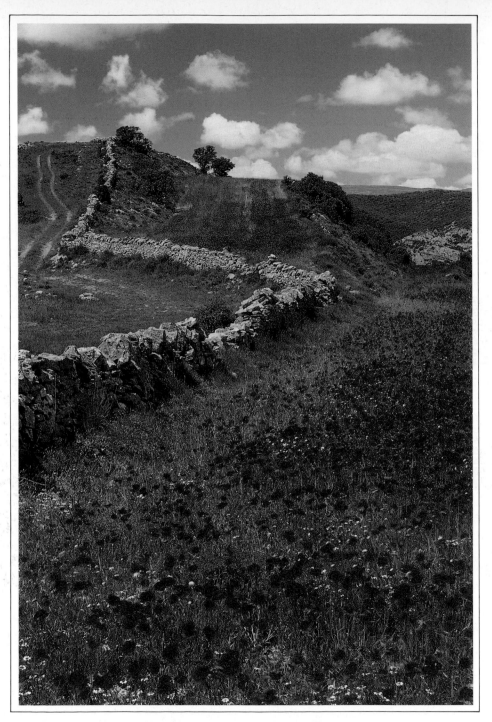

NEAR MIRAMBEL IN THE PROVINCE OF TERUEL

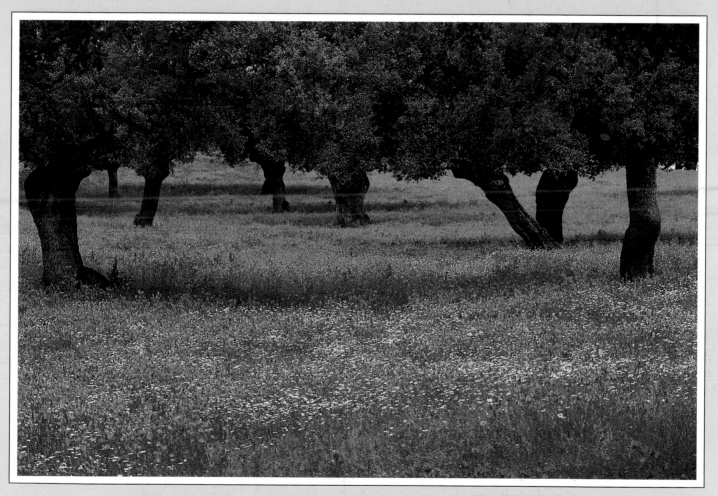

NEAR ZAFRA IN THE PROVINCE OF BADAJOZ

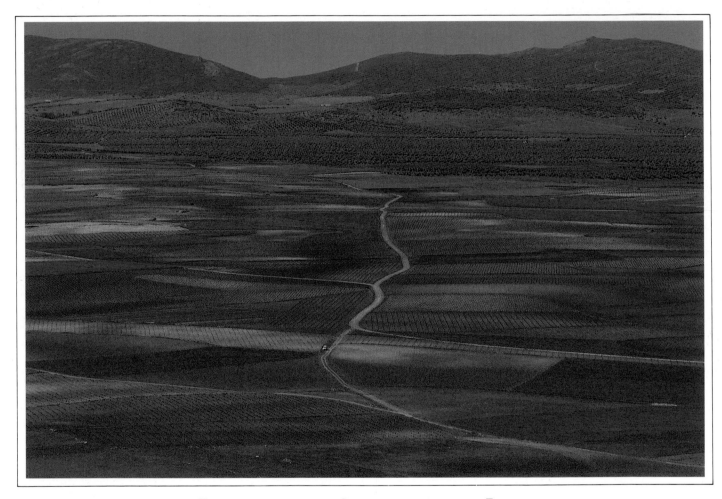

THE VIEW FROM THE CASTLE OF CONSUEGRA IN THE PROVINCE OF TOLEDO

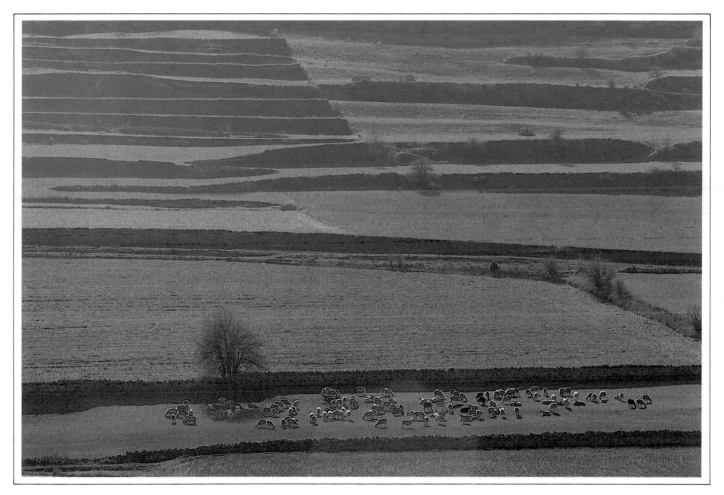

NEAR CAÑADA DE BENATANDUZ IN THE PROVINCE OF TERUEL

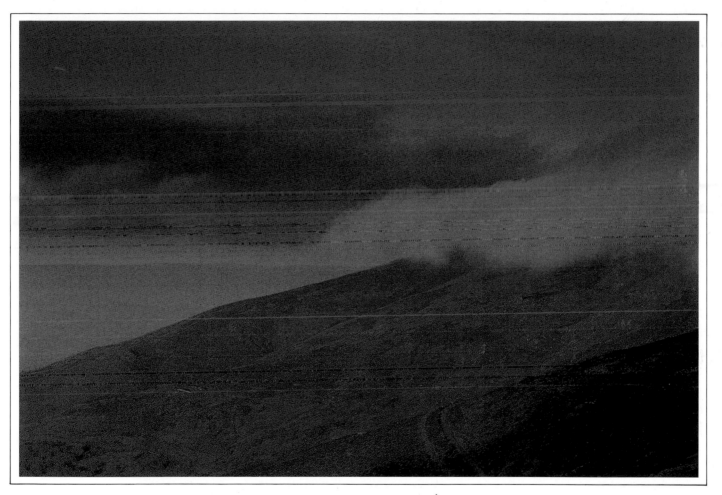

NEAR PIEDRAHITA IN THE PROVINCE OF ÁVILA

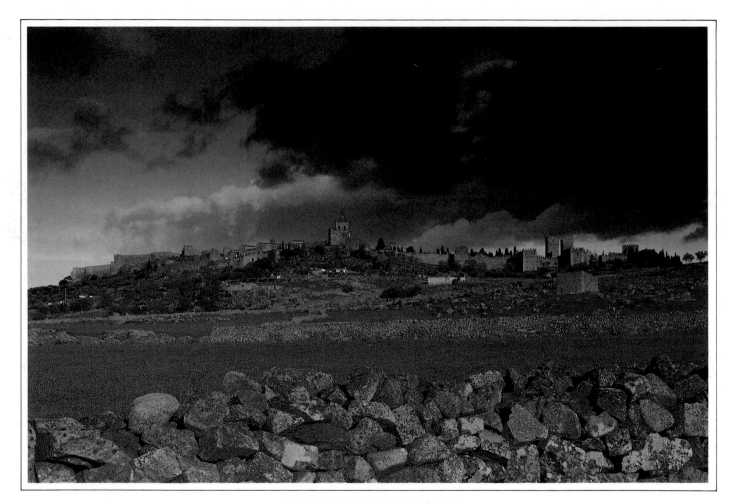

TRUJILLO IN THE PROVINCE OF CÁCERES

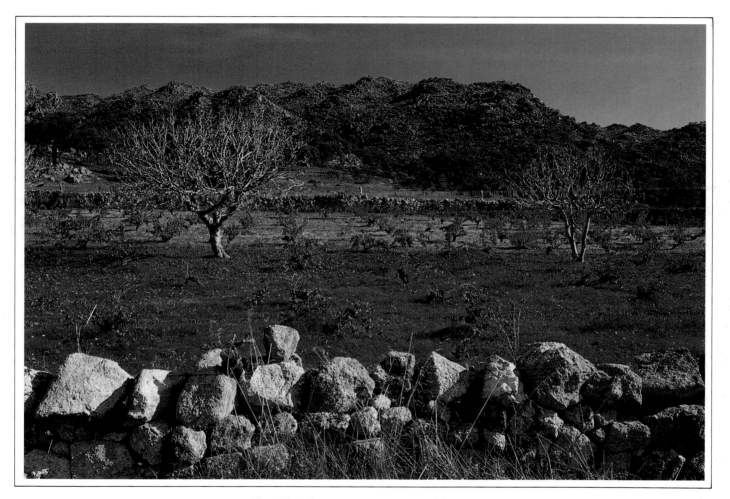

Near Montánchez in the province of Cáceres

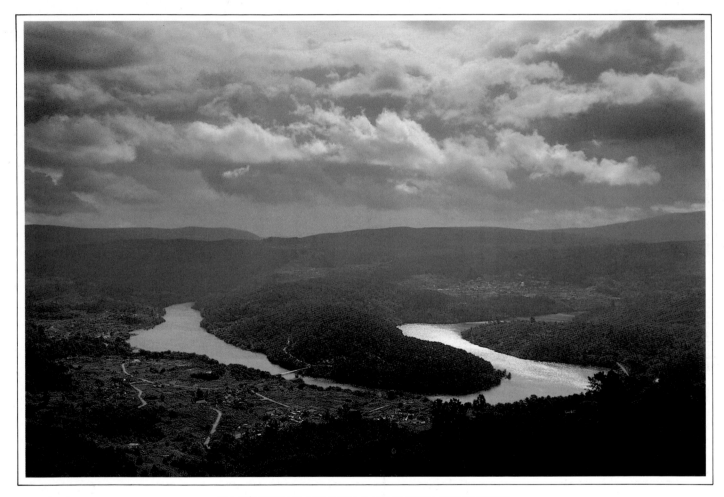

THE RÍO MIÑO NEAR FILGUEIRA IN THE PROVINCE OF PONTEVEDRA

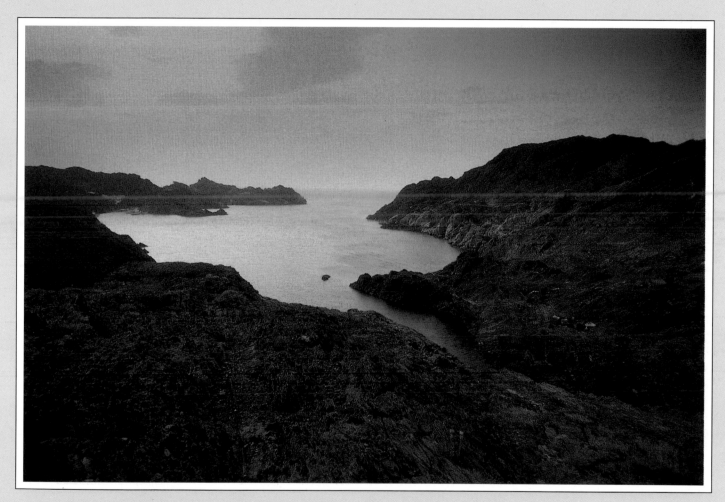

CABO DE CREUS NEAR CADAQUÉS IN THE PROVINCE OF GERONA

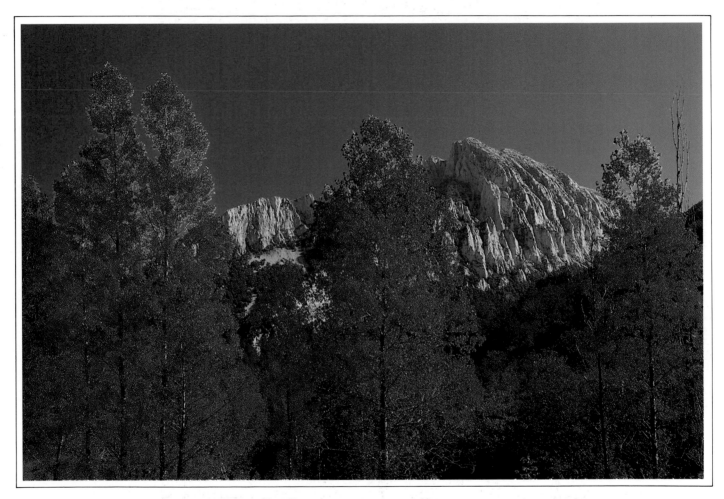

Near Roncal in the province of Navarra

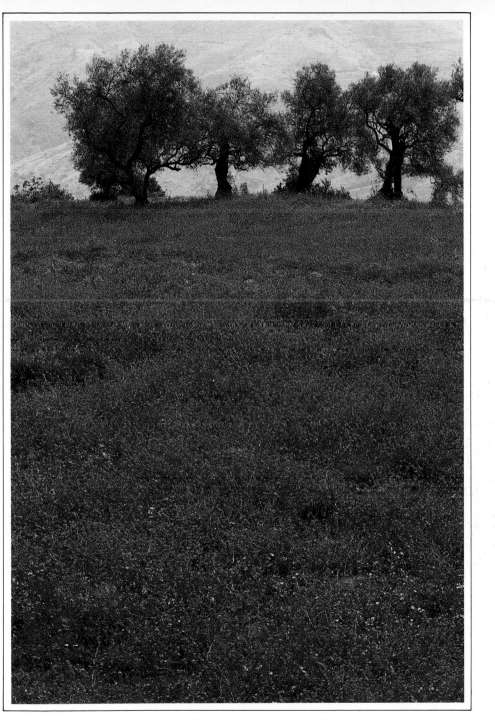

Near Vélez Málaga in the province of Málaga

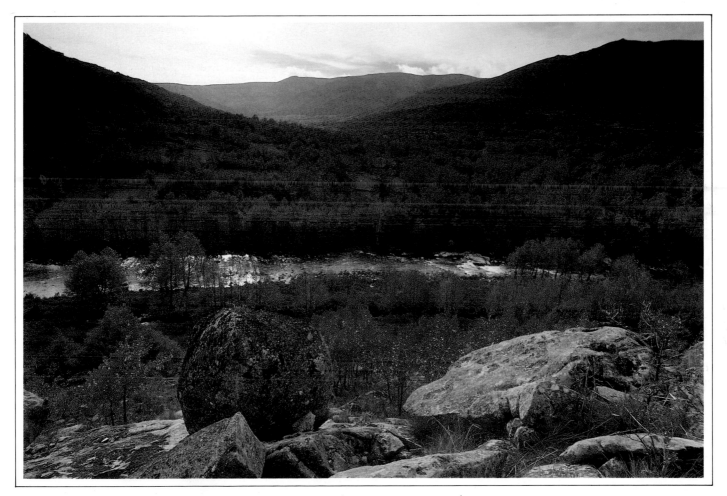

Near El Barco de Ávila in the province of Ávila

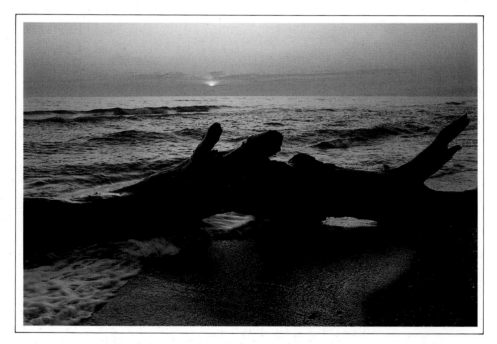

The beach at El Morche, near Nerja, in the province of Málaga